EXTRAORDINARY WOMEN IN HISTORY

*70 Remarkable Women Who Made a Difference,
Inspired & Broke Barriers*

LEAH GAIL

Cover Design: dezinir.99
Email: redbox5580@gmail.com

ISBN: 9798730231733 (Paperback)

TABLE OF CONTENTS

Introduction 1

Chapter 1 – Athletic Women and Daredevils of the Sky 3
    Alice Milliat (1884–1957) 5
    Bessie Coleman (1892–1926) 7
    Amelia Earhart (1897–1937) 10
    Lily Parr (1905–1978) 12
    Gertrude Ederle (1905–2003) 15
    Babe Didrikson Zaharias (1911–1956) 17
    Alice Coachman (1923–2014) 19
    Junko Tabei (1939–2016) 21
    Wilma Rudolph (1940–1994) 23

Chapter 2 – Women Pioneering As Innovators and Reformers 25
    Metrodora (200–400) 27
    Hypatia (360–415) 29
    Mary Anning (1799–1847) 31
    Ada Lovelace (1815–1852) 33
    Florence Nightingale (1820–1910) 35
    Mary Eliza Mahoney (1845–1926) 38
    Marie Curie (1867–1934) 40
    Grace Hopper (1906–1992) 41
    Dorothy Hodgkin (1910–1994) 43
    Mother Teresa (1910–1997) 45
    Marie Van Brittan Brown (1922–1999) 47

Chapter 3 – Women In Activism 51

    Mary Wollstonecraft (1759–1797)...53

    Elizabeth Cady Stanton (1815–1902) 55

    Harriet Tubman (1822–1913) 57

    Frances Ellen Watkins Harper (1825–1911)................................59

    Mary Church Terrell (1863–1954) 61

    Mary McLeod Bethune (1875–1955)...63

    Eleanor Roosevelt (1884–1962)..65

    Alice Paul (1885–1977) 68

    Rosa Parks (1913–2005)..70

    Claudia Jones (1915–1964) 73

Chapter 4 – Women In Leadership Roles.......................................77

    Hatshepsut (1507–1458 BC) 79

    Cleopatra VII (69 BC–30 BC)..81

    Empress Suiko (554–628)..82

    Eleanor Of Aquitaine (1122–1204) 84

    Razia Sultana (1205–1240)...85

    Elizabeth I (1533–1603) 87

    Queen Anna Nzinga (1583–1663) 89

    Catherine II (1729–1796)..91

    Empress Dowager Cixi (1835–1908)..93

    Indira Gandhi (1917–1984)...96

Chapter 5 – Women Achieving Heights of Productivity and Creativity.....99

    Phillis Wheatley (1753–1784) 101

    Jane Austen (1775–1817)..103

    Harriet Beecher Stowe (1811–1896) 106

    Clara Josephine Schumann (1819–1896) 109

    Fanny Eaton (1835–1924)...110

    Virginia Woolf (1882–1941)..111

Hattie McDaniel (1893–1952) 113

Greta Garbo (1905–1990) 114

Ella Jane Fitzgerald (1917–1996) 116

Gwendolyn Brooks (1917–2000) 119

Anne Frank (1929–1945) 121

Miriam Makeba (1932–2008) 123

Chapter 6 – Women's Contributions in War and Military Service 127

Boudicca (30–61) 129

Joan Of Arc (1412–1431) 130

Jacqueline Cochran (1906–1980) 133

Irena Sendler (1910–2008) 134

Noor Inayat Khan (1914–1944) 137

Nancy Harkness Love (1914–1976) 138

Susan Ahn Cuddy (1915–2015) 140

Lilian Bader (1918–2015) 142

Jane Kendeigh (1922–1987) 143

Chapter 7 – Women with Wanderlust and Conservationists 145

Gudrid Thorbjarnardóttir (980–1019) 147

Jeanne Baret (1740–1807) 148

Louise Arner Boyd (1887–1972) 150

Lady Grace HAY Drummond-Hay (1895–1946) 151

Aloha Wanderwell (1906–1996) 153

Rachel Carson (1907–1964) 155

Dian Fossey (1932–1985) 158

MaVynee Betsch (1935–2005) 160

Wangari Maathai (1940–2011) 162

Bibliography 165

INTRODUCTION

Throughout history, women have been quietly changing the world with their brilliant, curious minds, beautiful, creative souls, and courageous, passionate hearts. Now the time has come to celebrate women's achievements. To share the stories of those who have too often been uncelebrated. Women who fought, created, and adventured in the face of prejudice and hardship.

In exploring the influential impact of women, one of the most awe-inspiring features we discover is the audacity with which they embarked on their journey. Often ignoring the cultural and religious norms for women of their time, they left their marks in multiple ways. These intrepid women are pioneers in science, drivers of various movements, and harbingers of productivity and creativity. Their unwavering determination—often in the face of barriers such as injustice—helped them pave the way for others who came later.

This book aims to promote many women's achievements and seal their place in the annals of history. Each chapter focuses on particular areas where women's unique personal talents have significantly contributed to a field. These include travel, exploration, women's rights, politics and movements, literature, leadership, military service and pioneering inventions and discoveries.

Further, the book offers a compilation of the genius of women, their struggles and efforts in pursuing their goals, their determination to stand against stiff competition, and their admirable determination to fulfil their goals.

Our desire is for it to be an inspirational book for people of every age, gender, race, creed, or colour. Many of these women's stories provide stirring encouragement to our own lives. They can help us set our own goals and reinforce our belief in ourselves. They can help us attain the unobtainable as we strive to find our own place in the world.

CHAPTER 1

ATHLETIC WOMEN AND DAREDEVILS OF THE SKY

ALICE MILLIAT (1884–1957)

"The Suffragette of Sport"
The Woman who Pushed for the Inclusion
of Women's Events at the Olympic Games

Even as a child, Alice Milliat devoted herself to sport. Her particular passions lay in swimming, hockey, and rowing. From these early enthusiasms, she became a pioneer for women's sport—firstly in her home country of France, and later around the world. Alice emerged as a leading figure in the international movement for women's sports during the 1920s and 1930s. In 1921, she founded the Fédération Sportive Féminine Internationale (FSFI). She was a tenacious and strong-willed visionary who committed her life to highlighting the importance of women's sports.

Her greatest accomplishment, however, probably lay in her foundation for an alternative Olympic Games for women. When Pierre de Coubertin founded the modern Olympics in 1884, his vision seemed limited to men and upper-class men. Only athletes from this narrow field were offered the privilege of participation. In de Coubertin's day, women were regarded as the "weak" members of society, and sports were too "aggressive" for them. In fact, it was not until the 1900 Games that women could partake at all. Even then, their involvement was limited to a few sports, such as golf and tennis; participation in, for example, track events was still not permitted.

Alice Milliat raised her voice against this discrimination. She pushed for the inclusion of women's events in the Olympic Games. She believed sports gave women confidence and strength of character and nurtured their personalities. Alice was a bold and fierce woman. She would not surrender to men's misogyny and took an unwavering stance for womanhood.

Milliat and her peers created FSFI, which gave birth to the first Women's Games in 1921. She became the president of FSFI and took it upon herself to build an international platform for female athletes. The FSFI held a Women's Olympic Games, which would include all sports, rather than the restricted number allowed to women in the official Olympics of those days.

By 1922, thirty-eight countries from five continents were affiliated with FSFI, and it was decided to hold the "Women's Olympic Games" every four years. In August 1922, the first Women's Olympics was conducted at Stade Pershing in Paris. These games featured five teams, including the United States, Great Britain, Switzerland, and Czechoslovakia, as well as the host country, France. Despite dwindling funds, eleven athletic events were conducted, which drew a crowd of twenty thousand people.

Between 1922 and 1934, FSFI held four Women's Olympics, showcasing many talented female athletes and providing them with the platform necessary to exhibit their talent. By the final games, held in London in 1934, two hundred athletes from 19 countries could participate. And that is down to Alice Milliat's work, commitment and fearlessness.

She led a fifteen-year international campaign for the development of women's sports. Her efforts led to, in 1973, men and women earning equal prize money for the first time in a tennis grand slam and the Women's European Championship final in football, selling out Wembley Stadium.

There is still a way to go with sports, particularly regarding pay, but a French lady with a twin passion for sport and justice began the process toward equality.

BESSIE COLEMAN (1892–1926)

"Queen Bess"
The First African American and
Native American Female Civil Aviator

Bessie Coleman emerged as an inspiration to black women oppressed by the twin evils of racism and misogyny. Her voice, delivered through speeches and gatherings, motivated women to pursue their dreams. Her greatest achievement was to succeed in the white male world of early aviation.

Bessie was known by many nicknames: Brave Bessie, Queen Bess, and the Only Race Aviatrix in the World. She was a self-made woman who had started by helping her mother pick cotton and wash laundry from a very young age. She took on extra jobs, earning some spare cash, and soon could support herself.

It was from here that Bessie developed a fascination for flight and aviation. In the United States, African-Blacks, Native Americans, or indeed women had little or no routes into the aviation industry, but that did not deter Bessie. If the United States offered no way into her dream, she would look further afield. An opportunity came from France, where she gained sponsorship to join the Fédération Aéronautique Internationale. This was her first step toward becoming an aviation icon.

On June 15, 1921, she became the first American woman to get an international pilot's licence. During her training in France, she mastered stunt flying and parachuting, both of which required relentless valour and bravery. Bessie was a highly skilled pilot, a natural, in fact. Sadly, when she returned to the United States, gender and racial discrimination held sway over talent. Stunt flying or barnstorming became her only viable career options.

In the early twentieth century, women were rarely given a platform on which to flourish. However, in 1922, she became the first African American woman to fly a public flight. She was popular for performing loop-the-loops and doing figures of eight in an aeroplane. Her performances enchanted people, and she became famous both in the United States and in Europe. She toured the States, giving flying lessons and inspiring African Americans and women to learn how to fly. Wherever she went, she captivated people with her amazing flight skills.

But Bessie was more than a pilot. She was also a firm believer in the rights of women, Native Americans and of African Americans. At public gatherings, she gave speeches and showed films of her stunts. She showed her audiences that they could also succeed and demand their own opportunities and rights. She inspired women to pursue whichever career fascinated them. Bessie became a hero not only to her own communities but to the white ones as well. However, despite the demand to do otherwise, she refused to speak at venues which did not permit black audiences.

Then, in February 1923, her plane's engine developed a fault, and she crashed. Her wounds were severe, but she was able to fully recover from her injuries within two years. She did not let this incident put an end to her flight career. Being committed to her cause, by 1925, she was back to performing dangerous stunts.

Bessie's ambitions included owning her own plane and establishing a flight school to help other women who were interested in aviation. She earned enough money to buy her own plane. Then, on April 30, 1926, before she could lay the foundations for her flight school, she suffered another air crash. This time, she did not survive.

Her death touched many people, and around fifteen thousand people paid their respects at her funeral in Chicago. To many, the little girl who had welcomed the twentieth century by picking cotton on a Texas farm and had grown into a pioneer of the skies was an inspiration. A symbol of hope and liberation, a woman who endured all the trials and tribulations white male society could throw at her.

AMELIA EARHART (1897–1937)

"Queen of the Air"
The First Female Aviator to Fly Solo
Across the Atlantic Ocean

Amelia Earhart is one of the well-known characters in this book. Her passion for flying began during the First World War. She worked then as a young nurse for the Red Cross, based in Toronto. Her job was to help injured soldiers returning from the front. Some of these poor young men were also early aviators, and their stories fascinated her. She spent more and more time at the Royal Flying Corps, watching the young aces train. Then, in 1920, she had the chance to get into the skies herself. It was, to be fair, a small beginning—a ten-minute flight at the Long Beach Air Show. But it was enough. Amelia had already worked several jobs—photographer, truck driver and nurse, but now she knew what she wanted. And that was to fly.

Amelia was fortunate enough to come from a wealthy background—her father was a lawyer—and together with her own commitment and hard work, she could put together enough money to take flying lessons from the female pilot Anita "Neta" Snook. Earhart dedicated her time to the art of flying, studied everything related to aviation, and spent most of her time at the airfield.

Then, in the summer of that same year, she purchased a secondhand bright yellow Kinner Airster biplane. She named it *The Canary and* began her unprecedented journey, including her famous Atlantic crossing.

But that was a way off yet. She had other records to break first. These included, after just two years from her first lesson, flying to a height of 14000 feet, a record for a female aviator. That achievement saw her awarded a pilot's licence, issued by the Federation Aeronautique. Aviation really was not an activity in which women flourished in those days. She was only the sixteenth woman to earn such a licence.

Then, in 1932, she performed her first brilliant feat. Only Charles Lindbergh had crossed the Atlantic solo up to that time. Amelia became the second person to do so. The feat led her to pen her own record of the event. *20 Hrs., 40 Min.* is an inspirational record of her courage, valour and skill. She justly earned the title 'Queen of the Air.'

More records followed; she completed a successful solo flight across North America and set seven speed and distance records for women. Incredibly for the period, she was appointed career consultant and technical advisor to the Department of Aeronautics at Purdue University in 1935.

It was the thrill of the skies which did it for Amelia Earhart. In 1937, she set off on around the world trip. This time, she took a partner, a navigator called Fred Noonan. All started well as the twin-engine Lockheed Electra left Miami and headed east. Refuelling stops were completed, and by 29th June, the couple had reached Lae, on the island of New Guinea. They were almost a month into their journey. They took off once more, seeking the small atoll of Howland Island some 2600 miles away. This little outpost is notoriously difficult to locate, and the navy put two light ships close by to mark the target.

Several radio communications were received, but the last couple of these were extremely worrying.

'The plane is running out of fuel,' shortly after, 'We are running north and south.' No more was heard. Amelia Earhart was such a prominent figure that the navy searched for nearly three weeks to find either her and her navigator or at least some sign of their plane. But the ocean was large, and as July reached its latter stages, the search was called off.

Much speculation followed. Had they been captured by the Japanese? Did they mistake another island for Howland and attempt a landing where none were possible? Most likely, though, the plane simply ran out of fuel and crashed into the sea. Neither the remains of the aircraft nor this remarkable, inspirational woman have ever been found.

LILY PARR (1905–1978)

The Unstoppable English Star of Women's Football

The English women's football team is on a high. Recently crowned European Champions, they have brought home the first major trophy won by an England team since the men lifted the World Cup in 1966. During the post-match euphoria, several players laid the foundations of their success on the female players who embarked on a life in the sport (career, for most, being too strong a word given the conditions under which they played) during the impossible times of the twentieth century.

One of those women to whom the stars of 2022 refer is Lily Parr, who should be listed among the greatest footballers in the game's history. Lily loved sports. As did her brothers—she had six siblings in total. One of these was a fine sports player himself, with particular talents in football and rugby. For Lily, to be out playing with a ball was far more appealing than following the traditional girls' pastimes of her youth. Sewing and cooking were for others. Sport was for her.

Lily was a sturdy athlete and a skilful ball player. This combination allowed her to compete with and against other boys. But she came from an impoverished background, and when World War One erupted and the factories emptied of workers as men headed to the front, like many of her peers, she took up employment in their place. One of these factories, Dick, Kerr and Company, also ran a women's football team. One which probably became the finest women's team of the day. And Lily was their star player. She turned professional in 1919 and soon was playing in front of crowds of up to 46000, on grounds as famous and venerable as Goodison Park, home of Everton.

Unfortunately, the growing world of women's football faced a problem from within. Sort of. The men's FA, or football association. This was a remarkable group. To show the kind of prejudices it enjoyed, this group refused England's participation in all pre-war world cups, arguing (with a total absence of logic or awareness of the global game) that the home nation competition comprising England, Scotland, Wales, and Northern Ireland offer a higher standard of football.

If the association was not prepared to put England up against the rest of the world, then it certainly would not allow a threat to its supremacy from the women's game. Quickly realising it lacked the power to rule on this branch of football directly, instead, it banned its own teams from allowing women to use their grounds. The association's reason? As vague as might be expected. Women's football, it decreed, was 'unsuitable.'

In a flash, the opportunity for women to play before large crowds was gone simply because there were no stadiums where they could perform. No doubt, the jackets and ties at the FA thought their job was done.

They reckoned without a character like Lily Parr. The chain-smoking, five-foot-ten winger with her silky skills and hammer shot was not about to give up football without a fight. With domestic prospects limited, Lily organised a tour of America. Meanwhile, Dick, Kerr Ladies was renamed Preston Ladies and continued to play when and where it could. Lily represented them until her mid-forties, finally hanging up her boots in 1951. She scored more than a thousand goals. (To give some perspective on the scale of this achievement, probably the most prolific professional of the men's game playing today is Cristiano Ronaldo. He is two hundred goals behind Lily's total.)

Astonishingly, the ban on the women's game continued until the 1970s. It put English women's football behind much of the rest of the world. But for the likes of Lily Parr, it would probably have killed it stone dead. There would have been no European triumph, no women's Premier League, and no chance for girls and women to participate in the game.

In 2002, Lily became the first woman to be inducted into the English Football Hall of Fame at the National Football Museum. Now, she is properly recognised as a true pioneer of the sport, a woman whose playing skills were phenomenal and her influence greater still.

GERTRUDE EDERLE (1905–2003)

"Queen of the Waves"
The First Woman to Swim the English Channel

Like many of us, Gertrude Ederle was taught to swim by her parents. Mostly, she learned under the watchful eye of her father. These fine people also instilled in their daughter the lifelong attributes of tenacity, power, and confidence. Indeed, her skills, persistence and devotion turned her not only into a superb swimmer but also a symbol of femininity.

Gertrude was nine when she learned to swim, and by the age of fifteen, she had emerged as a significant international talent. Then, four years later, she won a bronze medal at the Paris Olympics (swimming being one of the few sports women were permitted to compete at those games.) In fact, between 1921 and 1925, she gained no less than twenty-nine national and world amateur swimming records. She broke seven records in one remarkable afternoon at Brighton Beach, New York. That was in 1922. By 1925 she was becoming renowned not only as a competitive pool swimmer but one who shone in open waters as well. It was then that she became the first woman to swim from the New York Battery to Sandy Hook, New Jersey, taking just seven hours and eleven minutes to complete the over twenty-mile course. Her record stood unbroken for eighty-one years.

Then came the endeavour for which Gertrude is most widely known. But before we look at that, we must consider a small matter which stood in her way (in fact, one which was a more obstructive obstacle than the seas through which she swam). It is a problem that illustrates just how hard it could be for a leading female sports player operating in such a man's world. Her coach in 1925 is Jabez Wolffe. Her goal is to swim the English Channel. Presumably, his role is to assist. She sets off on August 18th of that year. It appears Wolffe has an absence of faith in his athlete. First, he constantly slows her down, stating that she would not last at the pace she sets. When it becomes apparent that she is likely to make it, he ensures she cannot claim the record as the first woman to swim the Channel. She takes a rest, and Wolffe interprets this as her being in trouble, even though she is just floating calmly. He orders another swimmer, acting as a companion, to remove her from the water.

The problem is, it seems that Wolffe has tried and failed on at least five occasions to swim the Channel himself. It is speculated that he does not want his charge, with whom relations could be strained, to succeed as a woman where he failed as a man. However, Gertrude was not to be denied. The following year, aided this time by a coach on her side, she set off from Cape Gris-Nez near Calais, France, and swam to Dover, covering a distance longer than the most direct route. It was not just her swimming that raised eyebrows but also the scandalous two-piece swimsuit in which she was attired. Although, the layers of grease covering her as a protection against the chilly waters probably countered any allure offered by the swimsuit.

Thus, the reputation of the 'Queen of the Waves' was established; here was a woman proving that her gender could and would compete against men. In doing so, Gertrude punctured the widely held assertion that Channel swimming was both too challenging and too frightening for women to attempt. Not only did she take on the challenge, but she succeeded in it. 'People said women couldn't swim the Channel,' she later stated. 'But I proved they could.'

BABE DIDRIKSON ZAHARIAS (1911–1956)

One of the Greatest Athletes of the Twentieth Century

Mildred "Babe" Ella Didrikson Zaharias is celebrated as one of the great all-round athletes of the twentieth century. She displayed her talents in various sports, including such a diverse range as baseball, the javelin, the high jump, and, perhaps, therefore, unsurprisingly, basketball. However, it is as a golfer that she is probably best remembered. She even won an Olympic gold medal.

From a young age, Mildred set herself the ambition to become "the greatest athlete to ever live". Indeed, her sporting future was more important to her than her academic one, and she dropped out of high school to pursue her chosen career. Mildred began her amateur sports career playing baseball in her neighbourhood. Baseball came first, and her frequent home runs earned her the nickname Babe. Not for her feminine wiles, but after the game's greatest legend, Babe Ruth. Then, from 1930 to 1932, Mildred became a member of the women's All-American basketball team. All the time, though, she was adding extra strings to her bow, gaining skills that she would achieve in other sports.

Including the javelin. At the 1932 Olympics in Los Angeles, a 21-year-old Mildred won gold in the javelin, securing a new world record of 143 feet. That was not enough for this remarkable all-rounder. The very next day, she won another gold medal and set a new world record. That was for the 80 metres hurdle, and her time of 11.7 set a new benchmark for women in the discipline. She also, incredibly, secured the winning position in the high jump. However, her first place was challenged because of a technique she used. With a remarkable lack of transparency, the judges decided she could not have another gold but awarded her a silver medal. Strange that one would think that a person either had a legal technique and in which case Mildred should have received her gold medal, or they do not. If that is the decision, then surely full disqualification must follow.

Despite all her successes in the fields mentioned above, it was as a golfer that Mildred excelled the most. She won eighty-two tournaments throughout her career. In 1947, she maintained a winning streak of seventeen amateur tournaments. She also participated in the British Women's Amateur Golf Tournament and became the first American woman to win it.

Despite these records, Mildred's journey was not free of personal and societal hurdles. Women golfers faced a lot of gender discrimination in the 1930s and 1940s. Not long after her winning streak, she joined Patty Berg to co-found the Ladies Professional Golf Association

(LPGA) in 1949. Patty Berg was the president of the association for the first year, after which Mildred became the president for the rest of her life.

In 1950, Associated Press declared Mildred the Woman Athlete of the Half-Century. ESPN proclaimed her as the 10th Greatest North American Athlete of the Twentieth Century, and the Associated Press named her the 9th Greatest Athlete of the Twentieth Century. The following year, she was inducted into the LPGA Hall of Fame (now part of the World Golf Hall of Fame). Then, still, at the heights of her powers, tragedy struck. Mildred was diagnosed with cancer. She refused to allow it to end her career, and just three months after a colostomy—a major operation in those days—she was back to winning tournaments. But despite her resilience, determination and competitive fire, cancer was often incurable in the 1950s. At the age of just forty-five, she succumbed to the disease. But what a legacy she left behind. Perhaps most important of all, Mildred Zaharias showed that women could be anything they wanted to be.

ALICE COACHMAN (1923–2014)

The First Black Woman to Win an Olympic Gold Medal.

Racism was rife in the 1920s, in Georgia, in the deep south of the USA. That was the world into which Alice Coachman was born. But this determined young girl had a dream: to become an athlete. She refused to let the fact that the participation of women in sports was heavily restricted in those days—more so for a woman of colour—or end her

19

ambition. On the contrary, her 'can do' attitude and dedication toward accomplishing her dreams led her to make the best of what was available to her. She practised on her own, running barefoot and using whatever was at hand to improve her jumping.

As is often the case with people who break barriers, Alice had an inspiration in her life. While her parents were understandably reluctant to expose their daughter to even greater threats of prejudice and discrimination, others saw she possessed a unique athletic talent. These forward thinking people were her aunt, Carrie Spry, and her fifth grade elementary school teacher, Cora Bailey. Their enthusiasms were picked up on and developed at high school by a coach named Harry Lash. His expertise and his contacts saw her suddenly attract attention.

At the tender age of sixteen, Alice joined the Tuskegee Preparatory School, which specialised in training athletes. Her talents were by now considerable, and she secured the scholarship (no doubt with Mr Lash's help and good references), which she needed to benefit from the school's coaching. Now her career really took off. She broke the Amateur Athlete Union (AAU) high school and college women's high jump record. And did so while competing barefoot. After years of success, she won gold in the 1948 Olympics, her medal presented by King George VI.

Despite her success, Alice never forgot her roots. She established and inaugurated the Black Women's Sports Association to provide proper training facilities to those black women who faced challenges, barriers and rejection because of their race. After her retirement, she dedicated herself to educating younger generations. Later she was inducted into the Georgia Sports Hall of Fame. Then, during the 1996 Summer Olympics in Atlanta, she was honoured as one of the 100 Greatest Olympians of all time.

JUNKO TABEI (1939–2016)

The First Female to Reach the Summit of Mount Everest and the First Woman to Ascend the Seven Summits

Junko Tabei was a frail child. Back then, nobody would predict that she would grow up as a leading mountaineer of her time, conquering not only Everest but the 'Seven Summits', the highest peaks on each of the seven continents. What makes her achievements even more re-markable is that post-war Japan remains a deeply male-dominated society in which misogyny is an accepted part of life. Junko was not just a climber but a true environmentalist as well, back in the day when such socially aware beliefs were much less prevalent than today. She became the author of seven books, organised environmental projects to clean up the litter on Mount Everest, and led annual climbs up Mount Fuji raising money for youths whose lives had been affected by the Great East Japan earthquake.

It appears her passions for mountaineering were born during a school trip to Mount Nasu taken when she was just ten. It was her love of challenging herself in a competition against the natural environment rather than human opponents which inspired her. Allied, of course, to the chance to spend time amongst the beautiful mountains.

After graduating with a degree in English literature, Junko joined several mountaineering clubs, but she could not find one that could—or would—properly nurture her talent. That did not stop her from ascending Japan's highest peak, Mount Fuji. However, it made her realise that if female mountaineers were to have proper opportunities in their sport, she would have to do something about the situation they faced. Some men refused to climb with her, while others speculated she was only interested in finding a husband. They looked down on her for being a woman and joining a male-dominated sport. So, in 1969, she created the Joshi-Tohan Club, which was only for women.

In 1970, the Joshi-Tohan Club embarked on their first expedition and climbed the Nepalese mountain, Annapurna III. This was a huge initiative, as Japan had never had a woman-only mountaineering team. They successfully reached the summit, achieving the first female and first Japanese ascent of Annapurna III. Junko and another member, Hiroko Hirakawa, accompanied by two Sherpa guides, completed the climb to the top.

Next on their list is Mount Everest, the world's highest peak. It is not just the treacherous mountain that is presenting problems. Ascending such a peak is expensive, and most expeditions will be sponsored. However, the women's club faces the challenge of persuading sponsors—nearly always men—that a Japanese woman's place does not have to be in the home. With her usual single-minded determination, Junko eventually wins through, and the club can embark on its expedition.

An avalanche strikes them as they make their way up the mountain. Fortunately, there are no casualties, but the near disaster is another handicap to their ambition. Behind schedule now, they reach the final push. It is decided that only one woman, accompanied by a Sherpa, will continue. That is Junko. Forced on her hands and knees, she makes it to the top.

Junko Tabei showed both her Japanese homeland and the rest of the world that women can achieve what was previously assumed to be a male-only pursuit. If women can conquer Everest, given enough time, belief and perseverance, they can conquer anything.

WILMA RUDOLPH (1940–1994)

"The Fastest Woman in the World" Olympic Champion and International Sports Icon in Track and Field

Another successful woman who was frail as a child is Wilma Rudolph. She was a sickly youngster, suffering from both scarlet fever and double pneumonia. She also contracted polio which led to her wearing a leg brace. Nobody could have predicted that by the age of twenty, Wilma would be an Olympic champion.

Like so many of the inspirational women in this book, Wilma refused to allow her dreams to float away. By the age of twelve, she had taught herself to walk properly once more and was able to discard the leg brace. It was then that her natural athleticism came to shine. Within four years, she had been selected for the US Olympic team, winning bronze in the 4x100 metre sprint relay.

Four years later and four years stronger, she became a modern gladiator, winning three gold medals at the 1960 Rome Olympics. In fact, not only did she bring back three golds, but she smashed the world's 200m record in the process. (She also equalled the 100m best ever time and beat it in the final, but this race was wind assisted, and so the record did not stand.) As well as the two sprint events, she upgraded her team relay from bronze to gold in the 4 x 100m race. Breaking that world record as well, surprise, surprise.

If ever there was a person who demonstrated the ability to overcome adversity, it was Wilma Rudolph. She became a hero in the US, winning the 1961 Associated Press Female Athlete of the Year award.

Wilma retired from track and field in 1962 but did not sit back to live on past glories. Instead, she threw herself into the field of education and trained the disadvantaged at community centres. She also set up an organisation to train and support fellow athletes. Later, she was inducted into the US Olympic Hall of Fame. Then, in 1990, she became the first woman ever to receive the National Collegiate Athletic Association's Silver Anniversary Award.

Wilma contracted brain and throat cancer and died aged just 54. Her loss to athletics was immeasurable, and the world lost a remarkable woman. But her legacy remains. Her celebrity helped to break down barriers, her story inspired generations. She became an icon to black and female athletes and demonstrated that there is always hope whatever disadvantages we face.

CHAPTER 2

WOMEN PIONEERING AS INNOVATORS AND REFORMERS

METRODORA (200–400)

The Egyptian Gynaecologist Ahead of Her Time

The end of the Roman Empire marked the beginning of the Dark Ages, a period in a time marked by a lack of intellectual, cultural or scientific progress. But just prior to this period of stagnation, one person stood out as a pioneer of medicine. That this person was a woman, and her field was in women's medicine—gynaecology—makes her teachings even more remarkable.

Not a huge amount is known about Metrodora. After all, she was a woman! She was born sometime between the third and fifth centuries and was an Egyptian. This is significant. The origins of medicine are often placed at the door of the Ancient Greeks, and much scientific advancement from the hands of the Romans. But these were each extremely patriarchal societies, in which a woman's role was to be subservient to their menfolk. It might be an exaggeration to describe Egyptian society as a hotbed of equality, but the role of women was at least recognised; the genders were often regarded as equal in the eyes of the law. It was understood that women could contribute to the scientific and medical worlds. Not as absolute equals but at least as being able to play a role.

So, her birthplace aside, Metrodora's pioneering discoveries may have never been made. But they were, and that has been to the benefit of women over many, many centuries.

It is not just that Cleopatra Metrodora was a capable gynaecologist, midwife, and surgeon. She also wrote several widely acknowledged documents for their insight and organisation, with the oldest known manuscript of Metrodora's work located in the historic Italian city of Florence. Among her works, *On the Uterus, Abdomen, and Kidneys* is, and was, regarded especially highly. In many ways, her writings were forerunners in style and content to modern textbooks. Her works clearly explained many medical diseases and ailments that concerned women. They dealt mostly with gynaecological issues, including offering treatments for vaginal infections and highlighting the use of a speculum—an instrument which allows inspection of an orifice—for medical examinations.

Until recently, female physicians were doomed to oblivion, ignored by their male colleagues. But Metrodora's works somehow surpassed these barriers. *On the Diseases and Cures of Women*, for example, is presumed to be the oldest surviving medical text written by a woman. It is believed that the first Latin translations of the document appeared between the third and fifth centuries. Over time, other physicians referenced Metrodora's work and also republished it in extracts.

Metrodora was also a talented surgeon, performing cosmetic and medical interventions. These cosmetic treatments included aesthetic breast and facial reconstruction and re-suturing of the vaginal hymen to reinstate virginity for abused or sinful, "unlucky" women. To cure the foremost fatal of diseases like cancer, she suggested surgery for both breast and uterine cancer. So, sixteen to eighteen hundred years ago, Metrodora was sufficiently ahead of her time to understand the vital importance of removing cancers from the body.

It was through these innovative surgical ideas that Metrodora forged her way up the chain of medical fame. Her written works only enhanced her reputation. Her legacy continues to this day, with many medical institutions and organisations across the world bearing her name.

HYPATIA (360–415)

One of the Greatest Mathematicians and Astronomers of Her Time

That we know quite a lot about Hypatia, even though she lived sixteen hundred years ago, gives us a clue about her importance to our history. She was a mathematician, an astronomer and a philosopher. Possibly, she is the first woman to be a true mathematician. She grew up in Alexandria during troubled times. Her father was an academic as well––a well-known mathematician and astronomer himself.

Of course, these last days of civilisation before the Dark Ages swept many records of scientific advancement aside were problematic. Many of her works did not survive the period. However, records show that she produced pieces on geometry and number theory. She also revised her father's astronomical table, *Almagest*.

Such was Hypatia's reputation that she is considered the world's leading mathematician and astronomer of her time. She lectured to large audiences, and many students followed her passionately. However, her philosophical views were controversial during these troubled times. That, too, is a sign of how she was determined to follow her own path and ignore the restraints of convention. Alexandria, along with many other parts of the world during this period, was undergoing a bitter religious conflict. On the one hand, were the Christians, and on the other, the Jews. Caught in between were the Pagans, enemies of both foes. Hypatia was a Neoplatonist, a branch of the pagan middle ground. This belief system also persuaded her to spend her life as a virgin.

Education has always been a victim of religious extremism. When arguments are weak, an educated population sees through them. It was no different in Hypatia's time. The Bishop of Alexandria, Theophilus, ordered the burning of the Serapeum, a temple dedicated to a Greek and Egyptian God called Serapis. It is believed that the Serapeum held many of the books of the Library of Alexandria, a historical record of some of the most important thinking of recorded history. Hypatia was spared many of the worst excesses of the religious conflicts because of her reputation, which had earned her the support of Synesius, an important friend and influence on the bishop. During these times, she was allowed, encouraged even, to explore, teach and publish. However, when both died in or around the year 412, a new bishop ascended to the top of the tree of Alexandrian religious intolerance. And took it to new levels of bigotry. This new bishop was Cyril, and to him, a feminist figure of learning was a severe threat to his commitment to dogma and prejudice.

History does not record whether he was directly or indirectly behind the event, but a gang of Christian zealots caught Hypatia and brutally murdered her. Her academic achievements were already enough to secure her name for eternity, but by making her a true intellectual martyr, these murderers' actions ensured that Hypatia remains today a symbol of women's intellectualism, independence and intelligence.

MARY ANNING (1799–1847)

An Unsung Prominent Figure of Palaeontology

Mary Anning was born in Lyme Regis, close to the famed Jurassic Coast, a legend which her own discoveries of fossils caused to come about. Her family was impoverished. Her father, a cabinetmaker, called Richard, bolstered their meagre income by selling the fossils he found on the beach and in the crumbling cliffs nearby. The creatures her father found fascinated Mary, who was soon assisting him in seeking these prehistoric remains and polishing them to sell to the visitors who visited the coastal town in which they lived.,

In a life which saw little good fortune, the Anning's were lucky in that the West Country was popular with visitors from the home shires and big cities, especially London. These wealthy (mostly) men were fascinated with the landscape of the southwest during a period when war with France prevented trips to the continent. They wanted mementoes, and fossils were especially in vogue.

That was, though, the extent of their luck. Richard died when Mary was still young, and the family scraped a bare living from the money her brother, Joseph, earned as an apprentice and the fossils she could find and sell. Meanwhile, their mother kept the family together. Just.

Mary faced more than the horrors of poverty. She also endured horrific misogyny from the men, and they were all men who filled the leather armchairs of the Geological Society in London. These wealthy, lazy and dishonest individuals soon realised that there was a paleontological genius living in Lyme Regis. Except, although the facts pointed that way, to their narrow thinking, something was wrong. How could a woman, a poor one at that, be making such discoveries as Mary Anning? Especially when their own contributions to academia regarding this period of ancient history were second hand? They had a simple solution. One which settled both problems. They purchased Mary's finds, took them to London and claimed them as their own.

Mary's first major discovery was a huge ichthyosaur, initially spotted by her brother, Joseph. She spent many months carefully digging out the specimen, starting when she was just twelve years old. Her reputation grew when she added two plesiosaur finds: each of these dinosaur discoveries being the first of their kind. Then, the cliffs near Charmouth disclosed the first pterosaur found outside of Germany. These beasts were gigantic flying reptiles. Once more, the powers that be in London disputed Mary's find, even when presented with physical evidence of it.

It was not just finds of giant dinosaurs that Mary Anning made. Despite having little formal education, she made two discoveries that changed contemporary thinking regarding palaeontology. She discovered that coprolites were actually fossilised faeces and that belemnite fossils contained ink sacs, like modern cephalopods such as the squid.

Such milestones were embraced by the Geological establishment, but no credit was offered to Mary. Not everybody, though, wanted to take advantage of her. A keen amateur fossil collector named James Birch auctioned off several fossils and gave the money to the family. Henry De la Beche was another keen amateur geologist who also was a talented artist. His painting Duria *Antiquior—A More Ancient Dorset* proved popular, and he sold prints with the proceeds going to support Mary's family.

If Mary failed to receive the recognition she deserved throughout her lifetime, today, she is widely celebrated. Her work is displayed and honoured in the National History Museum, and a commemorative set of coins was minted in her name.

Maybe most movingly, in 2018, an eleven-year-old girl was so inspired by Mary's story that she began a campaign to have her name better remembered. Now, in Mary's hometown, a life-size bronze statue of her stands, hammer in hand, in recognition of her genius. A fitting tribute to a remarkable woman.

ADA LOVELACE (1815–1852)

"Mother of Computer Science"
A Pioneer of Computer Programming

We think of computers as a modern phenomenon. However, we can trace their origins way back in history, and one of the first computer programmers was Ada Lovelace, an English mathematician and writer. Her work on Charles Babbage's vision of designing an analytical computer led her to earn the titles of Mother of Computer Science and Founder of Scientific Computing.

Mind you, Ada had some creative genes inside her. Her father was the acclaimed romantic poet Lord Byron. Not that he had much to do with her. A renowned womaniser, he left the family home when she was still an infant and died when she was just eight. Her mother, who maintained a strict home environment, brought her up. Fearing that she may grow up with an unpredictable temperament like her father, Lady Anne would force her to lie still without even the slightest movement for several hours, believing that this would increase her ability of self-control.

Her mother did, though, possess a forward-thinking approach to education and insisted that her daughter be taught mathematics and science. Her tutors included renowned personalities such as William Fend, William King, and Mary Somerville, which helped unleash her hidden talent for digits and language. She attended the University of London and explored advanced mathematics while there. It was at the University that Charles Babbage, the father of computer science, became one of her tutors. Under his mentorship, Ada wrote notes describing codes and their functions. Babbage had a significant influence on his protégé. She was captivated when she observed him build a new mechanical engine designed to perform mathematical calculations. She was inspired to develop her own theoretical observations, including outlining *looping*. She compiled a list of the methods through which an engine repeats a series of defined instructions to explain this.

Through her work, Ada became a pioneer of computer programming. But despite her brilliance and background, she lived when the achievements of women in scientific and mathematical spheres were often downplayed. Often, her theories were rejected out of hand not because of any fault within them but because they originated from the brain of a woman. But this did not shatter her self-confidence as she knew she would leave behind knowledge that would help the world progress in technology. She was correct. In 1950, the notes of this legendary woman inspired the brilliant mathematician and hero of Bletchley Park, Alan Turing, which helped him design the first-ever 'modern' computer.

Ada Lovelace was a woman of extraordinary intellect. Her acumen let her touch heights of genius. Her passion and vision of technology-enabled her to pen theories and precious research through which the world could open new doors in the field. She was undoubtedly a powerful symbol of inspiration and ingenuity for women who have worked in technology ever since.

FLORENCE NIGHTINGALE (1820–1910)

"The Lady with the Lamp"
Fought to Improve Healthcare

Most of us will have heard of Florence Nightingale, the mother of modern nursing who tended to the injured—physically and mentally——of the Crimean war. What is less well known is that Florence was not just an incredible carer but also an incredible intellect. She was a curious child with a dominant personality who rapidly became fascinated with philosophy, history, and literature. Unusually for the era, her father took a significant interest in her education along with her upbringing. She quickly developed a firm grasp of mathematics and several languages, including French, German, Italian, Greek, and Latin.

Florence grew up to be not only a nurse but also a statistician and social reformer. It is, however, as the founder of modern nursing for which she is best known. Possibly this would be to the dismay of her parents, who wanted their daughter to pursue more of an academic career. But even early in her life, her caring outlook stood tall. She would monitor and care for the ill and poor people of her village, attending to her neighbours and helping them by using the knowledge she had gained from her father.

The family dynamics of the Nightingale home were complex. Her parents were clearly loving and ambitious for their daughter. Equally and not unusual for the time, they were also controlling. They tried to tie her into a marriage to a "suitable" gentleman, but none of their efforts proved fruitful enough to prevent Florence from accomplishing her dreams of becoming a nurse. In the end, she persuaded her parents to allow her to continue her studies and begin building her nursing career.

She applied to the Lutheran Hospital of Pastor Fliedner in Germany and was enrolled as a nursing student on her first attempt. Her commitment was obvious from the start. During her first job, she would

roam the wards in her free time and work extra hours. Seeing her affection for patients and her loyalty and dedication to the profession,
Florence established an excellent reputation with her employers while
her peers appreciated and valued her. She was promoted to the super-
intendent within the year of beginning her first job.

She also witnessed the unsanitary and unhygienic conditions at the
hospital, which were conducive to the outbreaks of diseases such as
cholera. Her determination to improve the sanitary conditions in hospitals saved many lives.

Florence also served in the British Army during the Crimean War of
1853. Leading a party of thirty-eight women in this dangerous environment was not a straightforward task, but Florence once again proved
herself. She arrived at the barracks' hospital to discover a place that was
filthy, with inadequate supplies and uncooperative staff. However, her
personality and intellect soon saw her managing and improving the
staff, whilst her commitment to the wounded soldiers reduced mortal-
ity. She ordered the dirt-encrusted hospital to be scrubbed inch by
inch. Her nickname was the Lady with the Lamp. She would move
around at night, checking on the welfare of her charges, carrying a
lamp. Her efforts were rewarded, and her name established. The government created the Nightingale Fund as a token of gratitude and
tribute, and her contribution to society included the first scientifically
based nursing school—the Nightingale School of Nursing. Later, during the 2020 Covid pandemic, emergency hospitals built and
equipped to deal with the expected inrush of patients with the virus
were called Nightingale hospitals.

Today, the world commemorates her birth and celebrates the importance of her services in health care on International Nurses Day. Who knows how many lives Florence's ideas saved and how many nurses and doctors her endeavours inspired?

MARY ELIZA MAHONEY (1845–1926)

First Licensed African American Nurse

Another woman who helped to change the face of nursing is Mary Eliza Mahoney. One of her motivations was encouraging greater equality for African Americans and women. Born into the free state of Massachusetts, Mary chose the life of a nurse from early in her life. As a teenager, she first worked as an untrained practical nurse. However, the plight of African Americans created financial vulnerability in them, even in free states. Mary needed to earn a wage to survive and committed to working at the New England Hospital for Women and Children. Not, though, as a carer. Instead, her job involved working as a maid, laundress, cook, and occasionally, a nurse's assistant. Following fifteen years of commitment, Mary felt secure enough to be admitted into the nursing school of the same hospital. This was in 1878. The course was challenging, and the work load considerable. Many dropped out, but not Mary, and when she qualified the following year, she became the first African American nurse.

Racism was, of course an unfortunate plague on American life, even to an extent in the country's north. Her thirty-year career was mostly confined to private practice, which was often used by prestigious families of that time. These wealthy patients were both fascinated and overwhelmed by Mary's skills.

Prejudice, though, was never far away. Mary joined the Nurses Associated Alumnae of the United States and Canada; however, bigotry was rife in the institute, prompting Mary to help form the National Association of Coloured Graduate Nurses (NACGN), which provided her with a platform to raise concerns regarding discrimination against African Americans. In particular, it brought to public attention the racism such people faced in pursuing both a nursing career and an education. Her activism was well-received in the community, which led to her lifetime membership in NACGN. This membership offered her a stage to highlight opportunities for minority nurses, and it was largely because of her efforts that the number of African American nurses doubled between the period of 1910 to 1930.

Mary's legacy remains alive even today. Several national awards testify to her excellence in nursing and her determination to improve the welfare of other minority communities.

Her work played a part in challenging discrimination and encouraging women from African American communities to follow their dreams, gain an education and embark on a professional career as a nurse.

MARIE CURIE (1867–1934)

The Pioneer of Radioactivity and Huge Contributor
to Finding Treatments for Cancer

Marie Sklodowska Curie's contribution to science and technology, philosophy, physics and medicine is surely one of the most significant and impactful involvements of any woman in any field throughout history. It can never be neglected.

Marie was born into a family of teachers who firmly believed in education and knowledge acquisition. Even they, though, could not have imagined that their daughter would become the first woman to win a Nobel Prize and later become the first person to claim a second such award.

As a youngster, Marie received advanced scientific training and knowledge under her father's supervision. She was a precocious child and was well known in her community for her personality, memory and intelligence. She won many awards, even back then.

But Marie was also dedicated and hardworking. She earned a first degree in physical sciences and then a second in mathematical sciences while all the time taking on additional work to earn her keep. Soon she was standing out even among the talented university students around her.

She married her colleague, Pierre Curie, who was also a physicist. They shared a love and passion for science, and together they formed a dynamic duo which brought about revolutionary changes in thinking across the world. The first area of discovery Curie made was in radio-activity. Indeed, she became a pioneer in the discipline. Together with her husband and another colleague, Henri Becquerel, they published their scientific research on radioactivity, for which they won the Nobel Prize in Physics.

Pierre died suddenly and unexpectedly, and Marie was determined to carry on her research and develop their work together, which they had begun together. Her husband's death also left a vacancy at the Sorbonne, and Marie was offered the opportunity to become the first female professor there. Later on, she achieved the isolation of two of the radioactive elements, radium and polonium, for which she was awarded her second Nobel Prize. This time the award was in chemistry.

Marie Curie laid the foundations for improvements in the treatment of cancer and also advocated the importance of x-rays in medicine. However, her years of work on radioactivity took a toll on her, and her continuous exposure to the dangerous waves led to her death. She will, though, always be remembered for her contribution to science and medicine and her role as an inspirational figure in encouraging women across the world to pursue a career in the sciences.

GRACE HOPPER (1906–1992)

A Pioneer of Computer Programming

Grace Hopper believed in saying things as she saw them. It was a char-acteristic which would see her achieve astonishing success in the developing field of computer programming, and become one of the first three computer programmers. Through this, she garnered her reputation as a pioneer of computer programming.

Even as a child, Grace was inquisitive. Born in New York, she attended Vassar, a private college in the city known for its liberal approach, where she gained a degree in mathematics and physics. Then, she went to Yale to study her PhD in the former. Her specialism lies in developing computer languages.

Grace was an enthusiastic patriot. When Pearl Harbor was bombed, and World War II started for America, she immediately took leave from Vassar, where she worked as an assistant professor, and offered her energy and insight to her country. Misogyny rules even in wartime, and initially, she was turned down, but this did not stop her. She persisted and applied on several further occasions until she was allowed to join the US Naval Reserve. Her intelligence was soon spotted, and she was allocated to a science project to be used to improve shipping. There she pioneered a 561-page user manual for the Mark I, an electrochemical computer. She also developed a programming system using punched tape for the early computer. Later she designed and developed the Mark II and Mark III computers and was appointed as a research fellow in engineering sciences and applied physics.

After the war, Grace joined Eckert-Mauchly Computer Corporation in Philadelphia, where she performed her duties as a senior mathematician and worked in UNIVAC I (Universal Automatic Computer) as a senior programmer at Remington Rand. She and her highly qualified team developed the first computer language, "compiler" known as A-

0, and the first programming language using English-like commands. This earned her and her team worldwide recognition and a fine reputation. Monitoring commercial opportunities, Grace and her team next turned their attention to the world of commerce and developed COBOL (common business-oriented language), which they could then promote in the public, military, and private sectors.

Grace Hopper is a role model for all modern computer programmers and for women across the globe who contribute to science and computers. Her impeccable research, considerable achievements and consummate aptitude made her a renowned personality across the globe and secured her place in history. Throughout her career, she was awarded no less than forty honorary degrees along with many scholarships, awards and professorships. She is considered a pioneer of modern programming, and President George Bush rewarded her with the National Award of Technology, thus making her the first woman to be honoured as an individual in this way.

DOROTHY HODGKIN (1910–1994)

English Chemist Who Played a Prominent Role in Researching and Working on the Structure of Penicillin and Vitamin B12

Dorothy Mary Crowfoot Hodgkin was born in 1910 to John and Grace May Crowfoot, the eldest of their four daughters. The family lived and worked in colonial administration in North Africa and the Middle East and were enthusiastic amateur archaeologists.

Dorothy grew up to become a chemist who played a prominent role in researching and working on the structure of penicillin and vitamin B12. Her outstanding contribution to this field led her to receive the Nobel Prize for Chemistry in 1964, making her the first and only British woman to be awarded the Nobel Prize for science.

Mary's parents believed in the education of their daughters and displayed significant support for their interests. Not for them, the traditional English Public-School attitudes of their time meant young women of a certain social class were taught to be excellent wives, handle themselves in society and play second fiddle to men. Dorothy's passion as a young child focused on crystals and their shapes. With the support of her mother, she opted to pursue this field in her studies but hit a social snag. Science was on the curriculum for English 'gals', but it was predominantly a male subject. In order to experience the best learning, they decided that Grace must study with boys, who would have access to better teaching and equipment. She won a place at Somerville College at Oxford and graduated in chemistry. She also had the fortune to be at the forefront of new ways of studying crystals. At Oxford, she became one of the first students to study the structure of crystals and organic compounds using a breakthrough technique: X-ray crystallography.

Grace was blessed with both determination and the ability to think originally and critically. She set up a personal laboratory to perform analyses on a set of natural history specimens. This became the focus of her interest, and her aim was to untangle the structure of biologically important substances and crystals. Then another hurdle arose. Grace developed rheumatoid arthritis during the initial phase of her

PhD, which worsened gradually to where she could no longer operate the master switch of the X-ray equipment required in her experiments. However, her resilience now came to the fore, and she battled through.

Grace's work in her field eventually led her to many awards, including a Nobel Prize. That she succeeded in the face of a debilitating and painful condition is a further reason that we can regard her as a genuine leader and role model among women in science.

MOTHER TERESA (1910–1997)

Albanian-Indian Catholic Nun Who Dedicated Her Life to Caring for the Destitute and Dying

A tiny figure with an enormous heart and indomitable energy, Mother Teresa became a true global icon during the 1980s and 1990s. This peace-loving woman was born as Anjezë Gonxhe Bojaxhiu and grew up in southeast Europe, in what is now a part of North Macedonia. Her father was of Kosovan Albanian heritage and was deeply active in local politics during what became the turbulent last days of the centuries old Ottoman Empire.

This commitment to social awareness rubbed off on young Anjeze, but her father died when she was just eight years old. She decided her own route toward helping others would come through the church, and as an adult, she became a Catholic nun.

Mother Teresa (as she would become) had spent most of her childhood deeply engulfed in church activities. She also took an interest in city news and politics and was a vocal proponent for Albanian independence. She gained these characteristics from her devoted Catholic family, who also had a firm belief in God and the importance of nurturing the poor.

Under her mother's guidance, she was encouraged to go on a pilgrimage with her church, and it was then that she felt her first calling to be a nun and devote her entire life to God and serving His people.

She spent time in Skopje and Ireland, then moved to India, where she attracted a following for her support of the poor, and determined to spread a message of peace and harmony in what was a very troubled country. She believed in nursing and monitoring the poor as a sign of her love and respect for God.

This selfless, passionate, and benevolent lady adopted the name Sister Mary Teresa before going to India and teaching at Saint Mary's High School for Girls in Calcutta. She proved to be a guiding light for her students and transferred her knowledge and insight to them. Sister Teresa believed in eradicating poverty through education and wanted the girls to be a helping hand and blessing for their families, who lived hand to mouth. To become a better teacher, she learned Bengali and Hindi, speaking both fluently, and guided her young girls in geography and history. Later, after taking further vows to dedicate her life to poverty, chastity, and obedience, she adopted the title of Mother Teresa and continued teaching at the school until they promoted her to the position of principal.

Mother Teresa was a beacon of generosity, kindness, and magnanimity. Her generosity toward Indian citizens was spectacular and admired throughout her country and across the world. Upon receiving her second call, to which she referred as a "call within a call," she devoted herself to the poorest people in Calcutta. These were the underclasses condemned to live in the slums. She worked tirelessly to build and fund schools and dispensaries throughout these desperate, impoverished areas. She believed that a combination of education and health offered the best hope of raising people's expectations and eradicating poverty and destitution. For her services toward humanity and her selfless personality, the Indian government awarded her one of the highest citizen awards, Padma Shri. Later, Mother Teresa was awarded the Nobel Peace Award for her humanitarian work and services. The vision of her, and there are plenty of cuttings online, as a tiny figure, old but still full of energy, are as uplifting as it is possible to be. Today, the world still mourns the death of such a precious soul. As do, especially the poor of Calcutta.

MARIE VAN BRITTAN BROWN (1922–1999)

African American Nurse Who Invented the Home Security System

Born in an African American family, Marie Van Brittan was a hardworking, committed nurse who worked at performing her duties and providing her patients with proper, caring treatment. By the time the 1960s arrived, Marie was a successful lady with a happy family made up of a husband and two children. However, something was wrong with this idyllic sounding life. Marie did not always feel safe at home. It was this that led her to invent and install home security systems.

Marie's idea was to invent a security system enabling the homeowner to check outside from anywhere in the house. This seemed impossible, but people determined to accomplish their dreams do not understand the word impossible.

Marie began her work on designing a home security system. With her husband's help, an electronics technician, she planned her invention. The couple started by making three or four peepholes in the main door. This way, people of different heights or positions could be seen on the outside. Next, they set up high-power cameras which moved on a slider from one peephole to another to allow people inside the house to look outside and see who was there. She added a receiver system allowing the camera's footage to be viewed in different places around the home.

The Browns realised that even this was not enough. Not all people standing in the garden meant trouble. So next, they installed a two-way microphone system which allowed communication between people inside the home and those on the outside. Fundamentally, Marie and her husband had invented CCTV. There was just one more thing missing. What if the visitor was indeed up to no good? So the Browns invented an emergency alarm alerted the police directly that trouble was in their neighbourhood. It took them three years to get their invention ready for patenting. But nobody before them had considered using technology to enhance security, and by doing so, Marie and her husband paved the way for the levels of household security we can enjoy today. They may not have envisaged how technology would develop, but their thinking allows this technology to help us with our home security.

Marie Brown's invention gained worldwide recognition and the predominance of security systems for homes and businesses across the world today owes its origin to the intellect and persistence of the Brown family.

CHAPTER 3

WOMEN IN ACTIVISM

MARY WOLLSTONECRAFT (1759–1797)

"First Feminist of Britain"
English Author, Advocate of Women's Rights, and Philosopher

Mary Wollstonecraft Godwin became a pioneer of feminism by introducing the concept of equality between the genders. From her writings, *A Vindication of the Rights of Woman* is perhaps the best known. Until the twentieth century saw women respected for their intellect and achievements and their allure to men, Mary was mainly known for her personal life and affairs, which drew more attention than her literary work. But now, she is acknowledged as the earliest feminist philosopher, and many modern-day feminists cite her work.

As a child, literature fascinated Mary. Despite the conventions of the time, which regarded women as second-class citizens, Mary held many radical views about the rights of women. The prevailing view of her day was that women were naïve creatures who could not make rational decisions and required supervision. Mary challenged these stereotypes and argued that women were equal to men and that even nature deemed it so. She believed that the only difference between the genders resulted from their education and upbringing.

These ideas of women as somehow less able than men were indoctrinated and solidified through the education system. Mary countered that if women were to be provided with the same education as men, they would not only make good mothers and housewives but also they would excel in various professions. This concept was novel in western societies and somewhat threatening to many men.

Mary was a great moral and political philosopher. Her observations were challenging. And, as we have said, unwelcome in many quarters. Although they held some influence during her time, when she died, it appeared they were buried with her. But as the feminist movement gained fervour in the early part of the twentieth century, her views and philosophies gained favour once more, and people could see what a forward thinker she actually was. Particularly relevant was her philosophy that women must have equality in education to achieve equality in society. Her book, *A Vindication of the Rights of Woman*, was reissued, and its copies sold well, even though it was by now many years after her death. The book outlined her philosophy regarding the equality of both sexes and gender roles. Her work was finally given the appreciation it deserved. Mary's advocacy for equal rights for women and her stand against conventional attitudes toward femininity each came back in fashion and were awarded centre stage by fellow feminists.

In time, Mary became known as the first feminist, one who gave birth to the basic idea of feminism based on liberal thinking and enlightenment. She demanded that women should be treated equally in all aspects. She did not back down in the face of adversaries and stood by her ideology, thus becoming a true inspiration for feminists and other women alike.

ELIZABETH CADY STANTON (1815–1902)

American Suffragette, Abolitionist, and Women's Rights Activist. Led to the Passage of the Nineteenth Amendment, Which Gave Women the Right to Vote

Elizabeth Cady Stanton is known for her role in the emerging movements and campaigns that sought to achieve better rights for women. She was also an abolitionist and changed the political and social landscape of the United States. Her efforts led to the Passage of the Nineteenth Amendment, which in 1920, for the first time, gave women the right to vote.

Elizabeth was born to wealthy parents in New York. Her father was a lawyer, from whom she learned much about the nature of the world and the society in which she lived. She observed the interaction between her father and other members of the elite community in which he circulated. In 1840, she married Henry Brewster Stanton, an abolitionist and lawyer himself, and he supported Elizabeth in every aspect of her life. This included attending the World's Antislavery Convention in London, and Elizabeth became enraged when she learned that many women delegates and activists were not officially recognised…for no other reason than their gender. She began speaking out on issues such as women's position in a misogynistic society and how women should be given a wide range of birthrights, such as the right to own property and to take child custody after divorce.

In 1848 Elizabeth, with the collaboration of her colleagues, organised a gathering at Seneca Falls, New York, which led to the much-acclaimed Seneca Falls Convention. Highlighting the oppressed position of women in society, she officially started the women's rights movement. By 1851 she had become even more active, collaborating with Susan B. Anthony; together they served this cause for over half a century. They addressed many meetings around the country and proposed new reforms that would improve women's lives. Elizabeth used her impeccable writing skills to pen speeches which made the suffrage movement an interesting option for the crowds she addressed.

It is astonishing to realise this from the position we find ourselves in today, but before 1860 women had no rights to child custody, nor could they own property or take part in business transactions. That was before Elizabeth put forward her "Address to the Legislature of New York," which later helped secure considerable reforms in these areas for women. Thus, Elizabeth gave women the rights they had been denied for centuries. Later, when the Civil War broke out, she founded the Women's Loyal National League, which pushed for the Thirteenth Amendment that abolished slavery.

Elizabeth advocated for the rights of women and slaves for almost half a century. She started several organisations which encouraged many fellow women to join the movement toward women's rights. She furthered the cause of much other minority and disadvantaged groups besides this. Mostly, she gave a voice to women and other oppressed sections of society. A voice which had been denied to them until that point.

The movements she founded gathered momentum. It is sad to say that Elizabeth died before her efforts really bore fruit, but she left behind an army of crusaders who soon gained the right to vote and achieved many other accomplishments. While her life is a story of continuous struggle and tireless efforts directed toward the causes about which she was passionate, it is also the case that today she is rightly acknowledged as a founder and a leader in the women's rights revolution.

HARRIET TUBMAN (1822–1913)

African American Abolitionist, Civil Rights Activist, and Icon for Antislavery

Harriet Tubman was prepared to put her own life at risk in order to do the right thing. She is one of the brave people who played an active role in helping slaves escape. It earned her the sobriquet Moses among her people. She was also the first African American woman to be drafted for war and served as a scout, spy, and guerilla soldier in the military.

Harriet was born into slavery and originally named Araminta Ross. She had a hard childhood, one filled with mental and physical abuse. At the young age of five, she was sold off to become a nursemaid to a baby. In fact, Harriet was sold many times and suffered consistent and wide-ranging physical abuse. She never lost her innate instinct to protect her fellow slaves. This first manifested itself when she jumped in front of a slave who was about to be hit with a heavy weight. This time she sustained a head injury in making the rescue. The beatings she suffered and the physical abuse she endured left permanent damage, causing her to suffer from narcolepsy.

Then she escaped, along with some of her fellow slaves. She was working on a Maryland plantation, and. with the help of the Underground Railroad, she made it ninety miles north to Pennsylvania. Harriet welcomed her freedom but knew she had to help her siblings, her friends, and other victims of slavery. Soon she was appointed as the conductor of the Underground Railway, where she transported slaves using the dark of winter nights to avoid being seen. Hence, she was symbolised as the Moses of the enslaved people. Despite all the risks and dangers in her job, Harriet broadened her activities by taking escapees to Canada. This was in response to introducing the Fugitive Act of 1850. This controversial edict resulted from a series of compromises between the abolitionist north and slave keeping south. It required that any escaped slave found in the north be returned to their 'owners' in the south.

Over time, Harriet became acquainted with other renowned abolitionists, such as Frederick Douglass. She is rumoured to have freed nearly three hundred slaves, but with typical humility, she downplayed this achievement. Harriet was an empathic soul who was aware of the brutality of slavery and the need to abolish it. Not least because she had been a victim of the degradation herself, she ensured that as many people as possible understood the indignity, the cruelty and the inhumanity of slavery.

She even fought in the American Civil War, hoping that this would emancipate black society from slavery. She first served as a cook and nurse, and later she took on the role of a spy, led an armed attack, and operated as a guerilla soldier. In the Civil War, she freed 750 slaves and was the first African American woman to do so.

Harriet was a prominent voice in the women's suffrage movement calling for gender equality and equal rights for women. She was the first African American woman to be honoured on a postal card and remained an icon of antislavery and a symbol of courage in America.

FRANCES ELLEN WATKINS HARPER (1825–1911)

African American Orator, Abolitionist, Poet, Temperance Activist, and First African Woman Whose Work Was Published

Frances Harper is one of the most influential women of the nineteenth century. She was an African American orator, an abolitionist, a poet, and a temperance activist. She was a powerful speaker who could enthral audiences with her words, the strength of personality and charm. She is also still widely acknowledged for her books and poems. As an early suffragist and antislavery activist, she raised her voice against the discrimination against women and racial minorities.

Frances was born the only child of an African American couple. She became a domestic helper and worked in a home where she was surrounded by literature. This helped to nurture her into becoming the strong woman of her later years. She is mostly known for poetic works. In 1845, she published a collection of verses and prose writings in her book, *Forest Leaves*. In her second book, *Poems on Miscellaneous Subjects*, she produced an anthology of poems dealing with various topics related to her cause. She frequently read from this book on her abolitionist speaking tours, and it found enough fame to be reissued and published several times over. This book addressed themes of motherhood, separation and death and contained the antislavery poem *Bury Me in a Free Land*.

In fact, Frances toured widely, visiting many towns and cities where she would give speeches and address people on pressing matters of the day. She was a fascinating speaker, and her reputation ensured she gathered large audiences. One of her early speeches drew a crowd of six hundred of her peers; this during a time when black people were considered property and enslaved, and public speaking of women, let alone black women, was practically unknown. These large crowds were attracted to her progressive views and captivating words. She was an ardent supporter of equal rights for racial minorities and women.

In August 1854, Frances delivered a public address on *Education and the Elevation of the Colored Race*. She then began a two-year lecture tour throughout Maine, working with the Antislavery Society. She also spoke throughout the East and Midwest from 1850 to 1860. Besides her abolitionist lecturing, she also contributed more to the world of literature. Her story, *The Two Offers*, was said to be the first ever published by an African American author when it appeared in the September–October 1859 edition of *Anglo-African Magazine*.

After the Civil War, Frances took the brave decision to hold several lecture tours of the South with addressees covering the incendiary issues (for that part of the country) of slavery, women's rights, and other sensitive topics. In 1872, she published *Sketches of Southern Life*, a series of poems that perfectly encompassed her skills. From 1883 to 1890, she worked for the National Woman's Christian Temperance Union and was in charge of activities among blacks.

Frances's determination to raise her voice in public and through her writings meant she emerged as a leading pioneer of literature in the black community. And she used this platform well, constantly challenging the oppressed position of black people, as well as women.

MARY CHURCH TERRELL (1863–1954)

African American Activist Who Advocated for the Rights of Women and the Black Community

Mary Eliza Church Terrell used a variety of media to share her message. In that respect, she was decades ahead of her time. She conveyed her messages through newspapers, speeches, published articles and activism. Those messages reflected her role as a leading figure against the racial discrimination and misogyny of the nineteenth century. Being a part of the growing black middle class, she used her position to fight the tyranny imposed on the rest of the black community.

Mary had good reason for her passion. Her parents were former slaves, which helped her see the prejudice of blatant white supremacy and the oppression suffered by the black community. However, a turning point in her determination to carry out campaigns against intolerance and discrimination came in 1892 when one of her old friends, Thomas Moss, was lynched by a mob of white racists. The reason for this appalling and criminal act? Moss was an effective competitor in business. Unsurprisingly for the times, the racists got away with their crime and did not face any repercussions. The incident itself, and the injustice of the outcome, infuriated Mary. It inspired her to fight against racial discrimination, which had, of course been going on for centuries and put an end to white supremacy.

Mary worked for the rights of women and the black community alike. She believed that if both oppressed factions had equal opportunities in education, business, and community activism, they would no longer be discriminated against and could finally gain some leverage in celebrating their own culture and identity. She became a determined advocate for universal education and the right to engage in activism.

Her achievements were manifest. Mary's passion for education led her to become both a professor and the principal of Wilberforce University. In 1895, she became the first African American woman to be appointed to the District of Columbia Board of Education. She was a prolific writer and frequently worked with black and foreign newspapers and occasionally with the *Washington Post*. In 1896, she became the president of the National Woman Suffrage Association, which promoted education and social reform. She travelled widely across the US and Europe. In Berlin, she addressed the 1904 International Congress of Women.

This articulate, literate and talented woman tackled a wide range of social problems in her long career, including lynching, the Jim Crow Laws, and the convict lease system. She was a true advocate for both black people and women and helped spread the message of oppression suffered by both groups across the US and indeed the wider world.

MARY MCLEOD BETHUNE (1875-1955)

American Stateswoman, Philosopher, Human Rights Activist, Educator, and Presidential Advisor Who Dedicated Her Whole Life to Uplifting the Oppressed Factions of Society

Mary McLeod Bethune was a staunch supporter of both the African American community and women and dedicated her whole life to improving conditions for the oppressed factions of society. This impressive woman is renowned for bringing about societal reform and enhancing basic civil rights.

She was herself the daughter of two slaves and spent her childhood years doing back-breaking labour. However, she could find an education for herself. Later she sought to invest that education for the benefit of the coming generations. Mary left Bethune-Cookman College in 1942 and spent the rest of her life helping others and tending to the social issues which plagued society. Her initial plan was to become a missionary, but racial prejudice prevented her from doing so. Instead, she opted to become an educator. Her aim was to provide a basic level of education to the destitute, deprived women and, in particular, the black community. She laid the foundation for her school at Daytona Beach using chairs and desks made of crates. The school, and its students, embarked on a magnificent, exciting journey and her school later became admired as a prestigious educational institution.

Besides providing education, she actively worked against racial and gender discrimination. Mary was the founder of many organisations which partook in civil rights activism. After women gained the right to vote in 1920, she led voting drives, like others of her predecessors, risking personal racial attacks. In 1924, Mary was appointed the president of the National Association of Coloured Women's Clubs (NACWC). Then, in 1935, she became the founding mother of the National Council of Negro Women. During the Great Depression, she played a prominent role in redirecting the black votes from the Republican Party to the Democratic Party, after which she returned to work endlessly worked for the rights of the black community. Her reward was that in 1936, the president of America named her the president of Negro Affairs of the National Youth Administration, a deserved honour for her indispensable efforts toward reducing, with the goal of ending, discrimination. From there, Mary became a highly regarded political name and was one of the leading African Americans in government.

But for all of her personal achievements, Mary never let go of her roots, never forgot her promise to the deprived people of her nation, and always stood up for equality. She held that rare and valuable trait of becoming a successful part of America's political elite yet remained within reach of the common man. On the one hand, she formed powerful alliances with other leading politicians, yet ordinary people felt able to approach Mary regarding their own social concerns and problems. In many ways, she was like a modern messiah. This selfless woman never used her power and privilege for her own benefit; rather, she invested it in the cause of the black community and women.

Mary enjoyed many achievements during her life. She held a strong reputation as a public speaker, and was a superb organiser yet never lost touch with her own immediate family. She was a loving wife, a mother and a grandmother. That was important to her because

whether advising the president of the USA, promoting policies of phi-
lanthropy or representing the NAACP before the United Nations, she
was at heart an ordinary person, an ex-slave, and a fighter for the rights
of the disadvantaged.

For Mary Bethune, one goal mattered more than any other: to promote
the "unalienable rights of citizenship for black Americans."

ELEANOR ROOSEVELT (1884–1962)

American Human Rights Activist, Politician, and Diplomat Who Advocated for the Right of Humans, Racial Minorities, and Women

Eleanor Roosevelt was a strong and influential woman in America's
history. She was the longest-serving first lady of America as her husband, Franklin D. Roosevelt, had a three-term presidency over the
USA, which ran from 1933 to 1945. Eleanor saw the role of the first
lady as more than being the president's wife and transformed that traditional position into one which advocated for the human rights of
racial minorities and women. She worked for many charities and was
a well-known philanthropist. She became admired as a powerful
woman in her own right. One with resolute will and determination.

Anna Eleanor Roosevelt was born in New York. She completed her
formal education at eighteen and made her official debut in society
when her distant cousin, Franklin D. Roosevelt, courted her. Between
1906 and 1916, she gave birth to six children. Along with being a wonderful mother and wife, she handled the external issues of being a

politician's wife brilliantly. In 1917, she could resume her own activism and work for social rights.

When the United States joined World War I in 1917, she offered her services as a volunteer. Eleanor was both a humanitarian and one who acknowledged the dire needs of humanity. She visited wounded soldiers and worked with the Navy-Marine Corps Relief and the Red Cross. In 1921, she decided she wanted to work for humanity on a larger scale. She became an active member of the Women's Trade Union League and the New York State Democratic Party. Later, during her twelve years as the first lady of the United States, she worked for a wide range of causes that supported humanitarian goals. Among these, Eleanor helped agendas in favour of African Americans, women, and the poor. She toured the entire country and, in doing so, became the eyes and ears of her husband. She gave him an insight into the worries, concerns, ambitions and challenges faced by ordinary Americans. Especially the disadvantaged ones. Inevitably, as one who challenged the traditional role of the First Lady, she made enemies. Her liberal causes were controversial to many elements of the mostly, white and male elite. She was subject to mockery for supporting the causes that she held dear, but she did not let the critics hold her back.

Eleanor was instrumental in helping the poor and the oppressed during the Great Depression People faced many issues during this terrible time, such as gaining access to education and, subsequently work, and Eleanor acted as the catalyst for change. She was instrumental in forming the National Youth Administration (NYA), an agency focused entirely on helping people ages sixteen to twenty-five. Her sacrifices and efforts shall never be forgotten.

After the death of her husband, she did not stop her volunteer and political work and continued as a prominent activist for another seventeen years. She was one of the key members in the drafting and passing the International Human Rights Resolution by the United Nations in 1948. She was also inducted into the National Women's Hall of Fame. Roosevelt served as the first US Representative to the United Nations Commission on Human Rights from 1946 to 1953. In 1961, President John F. Kennedy appointed her as chairperson of the Commission on the Status of Women. In 1968, the UN awarded Roosevelt one of its Human Rights Prizes in recognition of her sacrifices. In 1999, she was ranked ninth in the top ten of Gallup's List of Most Widely Admired People of the twentieth century. Eleanor was also included in *Time* magazine's list of the one hundred most influential people of the twentieth century.

Being a staunch advocate of rights and causes of the oppressed and destitute classes, Eleanor Roosevelt will always be the source of inspiration for women and activists. She earned her distinguished position through her resolve to use her position as a national figure for the betterment of common and socially oppressive people.

ALICE PAUL (1885–1977)

American Women's Rights Activist, Suffragist, and American Quaker Who Is One of the Main Leaders and Strategists Who Proposed the Nineteenth Amendment for Equal Rights for Men and Women

Alice Paul's demand was simple—equal rights for men and women—but she spent her entire life getting it legalised.

Alice was born in New Jersey to a Quaker family. She grew up amidst the suffrage movement, and her mother was one activist of that time. From a young age, concepts like equality of both genders in voting, education and opportunity in life were inculcated in her. Acting on these principles she was taught from a young age, she pursued her own education and earned bachelor's, master's, and doctorate degrees.

Later, Alice travelled to England, where she joined the women's suffrage movement. During this time, she met American Lucy Burns, who taught her the militant protest tactics. These included dealing with arrest on the political ground and taking part in hunger strikes. In 1912, after their return to the United States, Alice and Lucy joined the National American Woman Suffrage Association (NAWSA), and Alice was appointed to lead the Washington, DC, chapter. NAWSA primarily focused on state-by-state movements, but Alice wanted to coordinate change on a national level by introducing constitutional reforms. The differences in strategy between factions within the group led Alice and her contemporaries within NAWSA to lay the foundations of the National Woman's Party.

Alice continued to organise campaigns and marches in the capital, prepared to embark on hunger strikes and vehemently asking for equal rights for women. She, along with her colleagues, was arrested many times. Finally, in 1920, her efforts bore fruit, and the Nineteenth Amendment was introduced in the United States Constitution, which gave women the right to vote. This was a tremendous success for Alice, but her struggle did not end.

She dedicated her life to the suffrage movement, working toward equal rights for women in all fields of life. She powerfully advocated the importance of equal rights for women and made clear how they were being held back in the fields of education and business. Of course, her proposal faced many criticisms and considerable backlash; after all, her proposals were made in a country run by men. But despite considerable opposition, she continued her campaigns in Congress on behalf of the rights of women. In 1923, she drafted and introduced the first equal rights amendment to the Constitution. When the draft was denied, she turned her attention to international forums concentrating on getting the approval of the League of Nations during the 1930s and 1940s. She planned various strategies to get her drafts for the equal rights of women added to the Constitution.

After being elected chairperson of the National Woman's Party, Alice continued her activities for women's rights and an equal rights amendment in particular. She successfully found references and support articles in the preamble to the United Nations charter and the US Civil Rights Act of 1964. Alice was inducted into the National Women's Hall of Fame in 1979 and then into the New Jersey Hall of Fame in 2010.

Very few people have had as much influence on America's history as Alice Paul. She was a strong woman who believed in gender equality and was one of the pioneers of feminism in the twentieth century. She broke the old and outmoded stereotypes and norms imposed by a male-dominated society to promote a society where both genders could grow equally.

ROSA PARKS (1913–2005)

"Mother of the Civil Rights Movement"
Strived Against Racial Discrimination in the
Black Community in America

Rosa Parks is such a monumental figure in American civil rights history that she was even featured in an episode of Dr Who! Although, the aliens she faced in that were nothing compared to the discrimination and oppression she and her peers encountered in the US in the periods immediately pre- and post-war. Rosa's personal rebellion was, in some ways, small in scale. But in terms of its symbolism and impact on both attitudes in the US and the willingness of the rest of the world to turn its eyes toward discrimination, it was a monumental act. She became a source of inspiration for those who raised their voices against racial oppression. *Time* magazine named Rosa Parks as one of the 20 Most Powerful and Noteworthy Personalities of the Twentieth Century. To many, she is *the* most powerful personality of that century.

Rosa Louise McCauley was born in Tuskegee, Alabama. Soon, her family moved to Montgomery, in the same state where she grew up, attained her education, and got married. Alabama is, of course, in the Deep South of the US, and during her lifetime remained a hotbed of discrimination and oppression of the black community. Rosa and her husband, Raymond Parks, were active reformers and advocates of equal rights for the black community, which was why they ended up being key leaders of the civil rights movement.

After graduating from high school, Rosa became actively involved in civil rights issues by joining the Montgomery chapter of the NAACP. This was in 1943, and she served as a youth leader for the chapter.

While she spent a lifetime doing good works and promoting the cause in which she so deeply believed, it was on December 1, 1955, that Rosa Parks left her mark in history. Her mark of defiance may have been small, but that mark it made could not have been deeper. She boarded the local bus in Montgomery, and on this day, it was busier than usual. Rosa sat in the 'blacks" section, which was at the rear of the vehicle, although her seat was in the front part of that section. When a white person boarded the bus and realised there were no more seats, the driver turned round, saw the problem and told Rosa to move, giving up her seat to the white passenger. She refused. The driver kept telling her to move, and she kept vehemently refusing to give up her seat to someone just because their skin tone was lighter. Later, she revealed she was tired of always giving her seat up to a member of the white community. She was tired of being degraded as an African American woman and treated like a third-class citizen.

Interestingly, it was not in the city's bus company's rule book that drivers could demand a passenger give up their seat to anyone, irrespective of race. However, Montgomery bus drivers had adopted the habit of ordering African American passengers to give up their seats to white passengers when no other seats were available. If the black passenger refused, the driver could have them arrested by the police. The driver called the authorities, and the police arrested Parks at once and charged her with a violation of the Montgomery City Code.

On December 5, 1955, the day of Rosa's trial, members of the African American community in the United States were asked to stay off city buses to show their support. People were encouraged to stay at home, take a taxi, or walk to work. With most of the black community not using public transport, activists believed a longer boycott would ensue. It did. The Montgomery Bus Boycott lasted for 381 days and was an enormous success. It ended with the Supreme Court declaring that the separation on public transport systems is unconstitutional.

Rosa remained an active member of the NAACP. In her honour, the SCLC established the annual Rosa Parks Freedom Award. In 1987, Rosa co-founded the Rosa and Raymond Parks Institute for Self-Development to provide career training for young people. She received many accolades and awards, including the Congressional Gold Medal (1999) and the Presidential Medal of Freedom (1996). Rosa Parks' name is iconic in the history of the civil rights movement. Her act of willful but peaceful, protest caught the mood of much of the world and brought about a change for the better. It was both a small protest, and the legal ruling to which it led might also seem insignificant. Maybe it was. But symbolically, the lady from Alabama did something that made people stop, think and question. Why should a person give up their seat because a person of a different colour wants to sit down?

The answer, of course, is that they should not have to. Rosa's protest not only promoted the cause of the black community but paved the way for the country-wide movement toward greater equality which gathered pace during the 1960s.

CLAUDIA JONES (1915–1964)

Trinidadian feminist, black nationalist, political activist, community leader, orator, communist, and journalist who contributed massively to eliminating intersectional prejudice

Claudia Jones is known for the diversity of her political affiliations. These clearly illustrate her multifaceted approach to the struggle for equal rights that took place in the twentieth century. Born in Trinidad, she emigrated at an early age to New York, where she worked tirelessly as a devoted member of the American Communist Party until she was deported to Britain in 1955 because of the racial prejudice prevalent against blacks (and communists!) in the US.

During Claudia's time in America, her wide intellect saw her rise to prominence. Through her literary skills, she became the 'Negro Affairs' (their language!) editor of *The Daily Worker*, where she wrote theoretical essays relating to including women in public roles and eliminating racial and classist discrimination among people. The enactment of the Smith Act during the Cold War era in the US, which criminalised aiding or abetting organisations regarded as being against the government of the United States, but Jones and other of her comrades under threat of arrest and trial. However, Claudia viewed this as an opportunity rather than a deterrent and spoke out eloquently against the American justice system. Indeed, a justice system which deprived people of their basic civil rights might well, as she and her peers argued, be an oxymoron. As a communist and activist for black people, she worked for intersectionality—the recognition of discrimination—long before it came to be used in the common parlance; Claudia not only strived for the cause of women and against racial bigotry toward blacks in the US, but also she attacked the class system. As a communist, she also argued for the emancipation of working-class people. During her trial, she spoke about the humiliation faced by black citizens under the Jim Crow laws, which relegated them to being second-class citizens. However, her attack on "free America" and its justice system led to her deportation. She was removed from her family, friends, and the career she had made for herself after her epic struggle in the face of US-government sponsored discrimination. To have communist sympathies, or even to be suspected of having such, during those dark times in US history really was to face a genuine threat from the Government. Today, we call this period McCarthyism after the outrageous (and, it turned out, dishonest) US Senator Joseph McCarthy, who was the leading figure behind this political witch-hunt.

The Communist party also existed in Britain, but Claudia discovered that her communist belief system differed from that of the British communists', making the first year after her deportation particularly bleak. Her enthusiasm and determination helped her recreate a new life. She remained driven by the cause of fighting against the issues of race, immigration, and the problems of gaining citizenship in Britain. Because of her long-standing prior experience in confronting such issues, Jones rebuilt herself within the British community and soon became the editor of the *West Indian Gazette*, a post she gained thanks to her literary knowledge and writing skills. Working on the struggles of black immigrants and the oppression faced by them, Claudia drew her ideas from around the globe, where similar struggles against racism and colonialism occurred with disappointing regularity. It was during her time at the *Gazette* that she had the idea for a large celebration of Caribbean culture in West London, and that idea turned into the Notting Hill Carnival, which remains an annual event to this day. Claudia is often described as the Mother of Notting Hill Carnival.

After her death, her ashes were scattered next to the grave of Karl Marx in Highgate Cemetery in North London. The political turmoil and injustice which upended her life and career did not prevent her from reinventing herself in her new community. Nor from becoming a leading part of it. Like others in this chapter, and many more women and men around the world, Claudia Jones played her own part in helping to challenge the evil of racial discrimination.

CHAPTER 4

WOMEN IN LEADERSHIP ROLES

HATSHEPSUT (1507–1458 BC)

Known as One of the Few Female Pharaohs and the Only Female Pharaoh to Have Gained Complete Power

Male dominance, it seems, is not a new concept. Hatshepsut is an Egyptian monarch who may have taken on board all the regalia of a Pharoah, but that all her monuments and statues depict her with a male body and a fake beard seems to take the idea a little too far. After all, she is one of the most powerful women in the history of the mighty Egyptian Empire.

Hatshepsut was the daughter of Thutmose I and his queen. When her father died around 1492 BC, her half-brother, Thutmose II, was made the pharaoh with Hatshepsut as his wife and potential regent. They did things differently back in those days. Thutmose II was a weak leader who died while in his twenties. At his death, Hatshepsut's stepson would become the new pharaoh but not until he reached adolescence. In the meantime, Hatshepsut was supposed to look after the Kingdom of Egypt and handle its administration.

When Tuthmose III came of age, Hatshepsut played a cunning trick and usurped the throne. She named herself the new pharaoh and con-fiscated all the power that came with the role. She faced strong opposition but quietened objections by bringing peace to Egypt. At the same time, she argued that she, not the stepson, was the legitimate heir to the throne, which was deemed so in her father's dying decree. But for all her cleverness and manipulative skills, Hatshepsut was a woman in a man's world. Such things would not do in those days, and she had her statues make her look like a male pharaoh. She did not push Tuthmose III completely out of the picture; rather, she kept him as the general of her military forces. History has not always served her well, and she has been called the "vilest type of usurper" by many historians. Unsurprisingly perhaps, these are mostly of the male variety.

Yet she was a great Pharoah. Her reign saw Egypt rise to its greatest glory. Unlike the previous pharaohs, she did not instigate violence or wars. She believed in diplomacy and established relations through trade, which became an integral part of her foreign policy. Her claim on the throne was consolidated when there was a successful expedition to the land of Punt and people came back loaded with luxurious items and exotic animals.

Another accomplishment were the architectural gems that she ordered to be built. Much of this work is found in the city of Thebes, which lay at the heart of Egypt. She built processional roads and many sanctuaries. Deir el-Bahri, just across the Nile, is still considered a wonder in the world of architecture. She undertook a massive construction campaign as well. In Thebes, Hatshepsut focused on the temples of the Egyptian god Amon-Re. At the Karnak temple complex, she remodelled her earthly father's hypostyle hall, added a bark shrine, and introduced two pairs of obelisks. At Beni Hasan in Middle Egypt, she built a rock-cut temple known in Greek as Speos Artemidos.

Tuthmose III had evidently had his nose put firmly out of joint by Hatshepsut. After her death, he assumed the position of Pharoah and immediately ordered every relic of her reign to be destroyed. Tuthmose III had been waiting to deliver his revenge for his whole life.

Yet regardless of this more or less royal family feud, Hatshepsut can be remembered as a renowned pharaoh who displayed wonderful leadership skills. Her long reign delivered a time of peace and prosperity typified by the art and many buildings she had created.

CLEOPATRA VII (69 BC–30 BC)

The Last Ruling Pharaoh of the Ptolemaic Kingdom of Egypt

Cleopatra VII Philopator ruled ancient Egypt along with her father, her two brothers, and her son. Her rule over Egypt spanned a period of thirty years. Even today, over 2000 years on, Cleopatra remains an iconic figure in world history. One who influenced the Kingdom of Egypt and is known for her diplomacy and stunning public communication skills. Her legacy is recalled in history books, primary school projects on 'The Egyptians' and many a Hollywood blockbuster.

Cleopatra is said to possess seductive powers and irresistible charm, but if her beauty was captivating, her intellect was even more so still. She was well educated in mathematics, oration, philosophy, and astronomy. She showered her scholars with accolades and enjoyed their company. Cleopatra could speak many languages and knew how to capture someone's attention through her words. With her eventual fall, the last Hellenistic state ended; this followed three hundred years of continuous rule, starting with Alexander the Great.

One of the most notable features of her time as sole sovereign was her communication style and her skills as a diplomat. In many ways, she was the first strategic communicator, a role now essential in international diplomacy and politics. It was mainly because of her aptness in leadership and public communication skills that she delayed the fall of Egypt to the Roman Empire. In fact, she achieved more than this. Cleopatra influenced the foundation of the Roman Empire, which underwent a prosperous and fruitful era under the reign of the Egyptian pharaoh. Roman literature and arts kept her tales and myths alive, where she was described as the epitome of beauty and depicted as equivalent to an Egyptian god. Without a doubt, she is one of the most powerful queens in human history.

EMPRESS SUIKO (554–628)

The Thirty-Third Monarch of Japan and the First Female Regnant in Japan's Recorded History

Empress Suiko was the daughter of Emperor Kinmei and a pioneer among women who reigned in Japan. She proved that women could be great administrators and compassionate and thoughtful leaders. She ruled for about thirty-six years, a very long time and one which offers evidence of her political acumen. In the reign of Empress Suiko, many new reforms were introduced, and Japan flourished.

Empress Suiko was intelligent and beautiful. She was inducted into her future role as a princess from a young age. She conducted herself according to the Japanese code of propriety, which was highly prescriptive, and she was well-educated in other aspects of life as well. After the death of her father, her half-brother, Emperor Bidatsu, took over and made Suiko his wife. The throne then passed through his half-brother Yōmei and onto a relative, Shushan. Amidst all the power struggle, Suiko was named the empress regnant, and she became the next person who ascended the throne.

Japan had always been a patriarchy. Hence, the role of Empress Suiko in Japan's history is quite crucial. She reigned from 592 to 628, and her era is marked by Chinese and Korean reform, which in term led to a new age for Japan. Novel practices and systems were added to develop the nation. Empress Suiko is perhaps best known for introducing Buddhism to Japan. She had taken the oath of becoming a nun just a few days before being crowned as the empress. Many people followed her and joined Buddhism. In turn, this was made the state religion by issuing the Flourishing Three Treasures Edict in 594.

Other notable accomplishments she achieved include introducing China's democratic system to Japan, which saw the country's first *cap and rank system*. This system allocated awards and lands based on the sacrifices of people rather than their lineage. She tried to capitalise on the powers of the country under the monarchy. Empress Suiko even introduced the Chinese calendar in 603. Many Chinese and Japanese scholars were invited to Japan during her reign and transformed the country. Another outstanding achievement made during the reign of Empress Suiko was drafting a unique seventeen-article-long constitution. The constitution was not like the modern-day world's; rather, it had laws and a code of conduct for the officers of the state.

Despite everything else she achieved during her reign, Empress Suiko showed that breaking the chain of male rulers could deliver success. She was a wise and highly competent woman who proved her skills and wisdom by introducing new policies which helped strengthen the country.

ELEANOR OF AQUITAINE (1122–1204)

"Grandmother of Kings and Queens"
One of the Most Powerful Women of the Twelfth Century

Eleanor of Aquitaine was the queen of France, queen of England, and duchess of Aquitaine. She also played a part in leading the Crusades. Her social and political effect on the entire European continent cannot be overstated. Her position as the ultimate matriarch has led to her being referred to as Grandmother of Kings and Queens. She was also one of the wealthiest and most eligible women in medieval France and England. She is remembered as a savvy power player who was the queen consort to both Louis VII of France (1137–1152) and Henry II of England (1152–1204).

Eleanor of Aquitaine's father was the Duke of Aquitaine. She was well educated for her time, not least because culture and education were a family tradition for people in the Aquitaine court. Eleanor became well versed in mathematics, astronomy, history, literature, Latin, and music. She was taught many languages and philosophy, along with horse riding. She also acquired several artistic skills, like painting, sewing, and embroidery. She was named as his heir by her father, who then unexpectedly died, leaving her to adopt his title. Thus, Eleanor became the duchess of Aquitaine and probably the most sought-after bride in Europe.

Eleanor was a socially active and politically astute person. She oversaw her lands back in Europe and handled administration matters with tact and diplomacy. She is also known to have been a woman with a free spirit who loved arts and poetry. The most famous troubadours of her time visited her. Thus she became a queen who promoted arts and sciences, sponsoring many poets and singers.

Eleanor's diligent use of her position and influence to further political, cultural, and social purposes elevated her to the title of the most powerful woman of the Middle Ages. She not only became well versed in acquiring knowledge but also engaged herself in the administrative affairs of Europe. Her powerful political and social presence combined with her accomplishments in her personal life. Here she was an excellent, doting mother to her children, yet fulfilled her public engagements in a way which won her the admiration of her people. Each of these is unusual for a woman in her position, given the period in which she lived.

RAZIA SULTANA (1205–1240)

The First Female Sultana in Delhi and the First Muslim Woman to Rule in the Subcontinent

Sultan Raziyyat-Ud-Dunya Wa Ud-Din, also known as Razia Sultana, ruled in a way that has quite a significance in Indian history. Razia Sultana is known for being strong and resilient in the face of opposing forces. Yet, she was kind to her subjects and always listened to their pleas. She is appreciated for her excellent administration in the four years of her reign.

Razia Sultana was raised by her father, who accorded her the same rights and respect as he would a son. She was not discriminated against because of her gender. Upon the instruction of her father, Sultan Shams ud-Din Iltutmish, she was trained in the arts of swordsmanship, horse riding, and archery. She was a bright woman who kept her eyes on the things that mattered, unlike her brothers, who lived lives of excessive luxury and riotous drunkenness. According to her father's decree, Razia was supposed to be his successor. But the officers of her court did not share their previous Sultan's open mindedness and considered being ruled by a woman a disgrace. Hence the court unanimously voted the loutish Rukunuddin as their new sultan.

Rukunuddin persisted in making mistakes and displaying his incompetence, giving Razia the room to turn local powerbrokers and the general public against him. He was disposed of, and Razia, in 1236 she, took over the throne, which was rightfully hers. She ruled her people with kindness and justice, gaining approval and popularity among the public. She was religiously tolerant and advocated for progressive causes. Being a brilliant administrator, she made many wise decisions and judicious war plans. Her reign is known for initiating much new construction, due to which Delhi flourished under her short four-year rule. She also led many battles in those turbulent times and expanded her empire.

However, Razia failed to gain the loyalty of the Turk officers who dominated in her court. They held a growing contempt for her, most probably because not only was she a woman, but she also appointed many non-Turk people to high posts. These obstructions were why her reign was limited to only four years. The governor of Bhatinda, Malik

Ikhtiar-ud-din Altunia, and Razia's childhood friend, first started a rebellion against her. She raised an army against him but lost the battle and was taken prisoner by Altunia. Bahram Shah, her brother, then usurped her and took the throne. However, this did not deter Razia from attempting to reclaim her rightful place once more. She joined hands with the leader of the rebels who had first captured her, Ikhtiar-ud-din Altunia—whom she married later—and tried to take back what was hers. Razia successfully assembled an army comprising Khokhars, Jats, Rajputs, and Turk officers, but her soldiers abandoned her on the battlefield and thus, faced defeat.

Despite her brief reign, Razia Sultana remains the only female sultan of Delhi and the first Muslim woman ruler to take over the throne. Carrying on the legacy of her hard-working, just, and kind father, she is an inspiration to many present-day women, as her life is a model to those who believe in standing up for their rights, irrespective of gender.

ELIZABETH I (1533–1603)

Former Queen of England and Ireland, known as One of the Greatest Monarchs in the History of Britain

Elizabeth I was Queen of England and Ireland from 1558 to 1603. Her rule is famed because it marks a time when Britain prospered, and its dignity was regained following the unstable time which marked the reigns of Henry VIII right up to Elizabeth's period of rule. She was given a host of nicknames and is often referred to as Good Queen Bess, the Virgin Queen, and Gloriana.

Elizabeth was the daughter of King Henry VIII and Anne Boleyn, his second wife. For three years, she lived the life of luxury, based mostly at Hatfield House, under the care of a doting mother. Who was, of course, famously executed. Matters rapidly descended into chaos. She was given a host of governesses, the awkward Thomas Cromwell, who enjoyed the king's favour at that point, withdrew money from her household to such an extent that she could not even be given new clothes, and she lost her status as a Princess. Worst of all, her half sister Mary was moved into the House with her, and the two rarely got along. However, Elizabeth had talents. She excelled at painting, music, education, and languages.

The throne passed to her half-brother, sister- and brother-in-law before she was crowned in 1558. Her coronation started a golden time for the British monarchy. Elizabeth was an intellectual who influenced and changed history. During her reign, the arts and literature flourished. Her latter years on the throne coincided with, for example, Shakespeare's most productive period. Many artists and writers came under the patronage of Elizabeth's court. She encouraged her nation's exploration of the world by discovering new places. This was done to explore new trading routes and expand her kingdom. Of course, the unplanned downside of this was that the end of her reign saw the East India Company formed, an organisation which caused harm throughout the world. It also marked the beginning of the British involvement in the slave trade.

Yet despite this, Elizabeth made England stable and peaceful. She inherited a bankrupt nation but adopted frugal policies and paid off the debt. Elizabeth passed the vital Religious Settlement, which checked the religious riots and protests causing unrest across England. The Spanish Armada, a great fleet of around 130 ships, 8,000 sailors, and 18,000 soldiers, set sail in 1558 to invade England and overthrow the Queen. Despite having a small naval force, Elizabeth won an astonishing battle. Some historians still consider this as Britain's greatest ever military victory.

Elizabeth I's reign undeniably marked a golden time in England's history. She crushed many rebellions, avoided expensive wars, and ousted conspiracies. She ascended the throne during a time of religious conflict and handled the situation with poise and ease. She returned the nation's pride and turned her nation into one of the most powerful forces in Europe. Her legacy is not perfect, but then she could not have predicted the worst excesses of British imperialism, which were to follow her own death.

QUEEN ANNA NZINGA (1583–1663)

One of the Great Women Rulers of Africa Who Fought Against the Slave Trade and European Influence in the Seventeenth Century

Queen Anna Nzinga of Angola was famed for being an astute diplomat and visionary military leader. She resisted Portuguese colonisation and slave raids for thirty long years.

The states of Central Africa became centres of economic power in the sixteenth-and seventeenth centuries because of the slave trade. Of course, the slave trade was morally corrupt, socially wrong and inhumane. Changes in the order of the New World led to demand, and it was the nations of central and western Africa which met that demand. Some African rulers embarked on slave trading of their own, but Queen Nzinga resisted this evil. However, her nation, like many others, became subject to European threat, particularly from the Portuguese, who aimed at gaining territorial control of the African region. While many leaders of the African states succumbed to this new order threatened by European and some native African raiders, Nzinga could overcome these difficulties and resist any colonisation threatened by the Portuguese.

Queen Nzinga reigned when the area was also under attack by native aggressors who often worked with the hated European foe. Because of her visionary insight, she could appear to align herself with Portugal while simultaneously repositioning Ngondo, an area which included parts of Angola, as a united front against their African enemies. Presenting Ngondo as an intermediary in the slave trade, Nzinga could end Portuguese slave raiding in the kingdom. This was a remarkable fete of necessary political skulduggery.

However, Portugal failed to honour its agreement with Queen Nzinga, and this betrayal forced her to flee, along with her people, and form a new kingdom at Matamba, which lay outside the reach of the Portuguese. Queen Nzinga used the military power of the new kingdom to form a militia which provided a sanctuary to runaway slaves and Portuguese-trained African soldiers. The queen could also form an alliance with the region of Ngondo to rebel against the puppet Portuguese ruler who had been given power there. However, their combined forces could not move the Portuguese out of the region, and the queen was once more forced to retreat to her stronghold. From this point onward, Queen Nzinga focused on making Matamba a trading hub and gateway to Central Africa. During her thirty-year rule, she could make Matamba a commercial state, turning it to into an equal with the might of the colonial Portuguese.

When European countries were spreading far-reaching tentacles into other continents and stripping nations of their most valuable resource, their people, through the slave trade, Queen Nzinga provided true and determined opposition to their imperialism.

CATHERINE II (1729–1796)

Russian Monarch, Holding the Title of the Longest-Ruling Female Empress of Russia

Catherine II is celebrated as an empress who merged Russia's position in Europe and made it a social and political force among the major powers on the continent. She expanded the boundaries of Russia and turned it into one of the key monarchies in the whole of Europe.

Catherine the Great—in Russian Yekaterina Velikaya—was originally named Sophie Friederike Auguste. She was a minor German princess from a tiny dominion in Prussia called Anhalt-Zerbst. Her father was its ruler. Her governess raised her while her mother paid attention to her brother. On December 25, 1761, Catherine II became empress consort of Russia when her husband, Peter III of Russia, died. He had taken the throne following the death of Elizabeth of Russia. Peter had barely ruled for six months when Catherine orchestrated a coup d'état and overthrew him, becoming the empress of her adopted nation on July 9, 1762. Catherine had conspired with powerful allies to carry out this coup. She was a shrewd woman who knew how to play her cards. She had stood up for herself and bring about change.

Catherine is sometimes depicted as a powerful but divisive leader. Europeans regarded her as a menace for proliferating into other regions and strengthening her nation. However, she proved that women can be great rulers; but there is more to her than just her political and military acumen. She was also a leader who actually cared about her people.

Catherine ruled Russia for almost thirty-four years, during which her nation flourished. She declared wars on the Ottoman Empire—the strongest Muslim Empire in history—to gain access to a port to the south of the Russian bear. Catherine delivered massive blows and defeated the Ottomans in many battles. She even captured new regions––sometimes through conquest and sometimes with diplomacy. At the end of her reign, two hundred thousand square miles had been added to Russia. But her interests were not just expansionist. She introduced many educational and administrative reforms that helped Russia become stronger as a nation. Catherine became the first monarch to find an educational institution for women. Under her rule, arts and science thrived.

Catherine also opened many schools across the nation, offering free classes to every child. She founded several hospitals, orphanages, and institutions for social care. She divided Russia into provinces and districts and passed administrative reforms which increased trade and improved communication. Russia underwent a transformation in every aspect under her rule. Catherine is also known for playing a significant role in the Russian Enlightenment, a movement that dominated intellectual and philosophical thought in Europe. She devised internal reforms and drafted a constitution that protected the rights of her people.

She truly was a prominent leader in the history of a mighty nation.

EMPRESS DOWAGER CIXI (1835–1908)

Chinese Empress and Regnant of China Who Led Her Entire Country into an Age of Development

Empress Dowager Cixi reigned in China for almost forty-seven years. She belonged to the Qing Dynasty and is famous for guiding China into a period of modernisation. During this time, she introduced several Western customs. Her influence over other leaders was considerable: she came into power at a young age, maintaining it over her entire vast nation and acting as consort to Emperor Xianfeng (reigned 1850–1861). She was also the mother of Emperor Tongzhi (reigned 1861–1875) and became the adoptive mother to Emperor Guangxu. Dowager Cixi oversaw the royal House of Manchu and became one of the most powerful women in the history of her country. Her impact on China's history and development is considered massive to this day.

She was born with no great prospects, as she belonged to an ethnic minority. No one could have guessed that this girl would use her unyielding determination and intellect to become empress dowager for almost half a century. Her parents were government employees, so she had no aristocratic blood. Everything she would achieve came from her own strength of character. Like other girls in China, her education focused around learning the skills needed to serve men, and she was apt at cooking, painting, sewing, and suchlike. At this time, China still operated a system of concubines. These were a sort of official mistress whose job was to serve the man to whom she was passed. A concubine lived within the wider household of the most powerful men but held a lower status than that of a wife. Such were the customs in China that when the future Empress Dowager Cixi was sent off to become a concubine to Emperor Xianfeng, it was considered quite an honour for her and her family.

The mid-1800s was a time in which many European nations were seeking to expand their interests in the East. In 1860, France and Britain attacked China, and the emperor fled. He died the following year. He had selected eight people to advise and guide his heir, Tongzhi. Being the mother of the new emperor gave Dowager Cixi a strong position in court, and she learned how to pull strings and stay in power.

After her son died of smallpox, Emperor Guangxu, Dowager Cixi's nephew, came into power. However, since Guangxu was only four, he need a regent to rule for him. Unsurprisingly, given her position in court, which was the Dowager Cixi, who also adopted her nephew to be her son. Even when Guangxu came of age and became Emperor proper, the actual power in China was still wielded by the Dowager.

There is much secrecy around China's ruling dynasty of this time, but it is believed that the court approached the Dowager over the most serious matters, whilst the Emperor largely presided over ceremonial events. This became, even more, the case in 1898, when Dowager Cixi staged a bloodless coup and officially retook her position on the main throne. Guangxu sat by her side, however. During her reign, the Dowager ensured huge developments were made in China regarding construction and technological progress. Chinese people were conventional, and their traditional culture was strong. They viewed change with scepticism and Western traditions as barbaric. But Dowager Cixi took the risk of outcry and still modernised China, albeit not completely.

She built the Railway Road in such a way that it would not disrupt the temples in its path. She started the second wave of modernisation and introduced coal power and electricity. Dowager Cixi declared war on France to challenge their claim on the land between China and Vietnam. She announced that China would turn into a constitutional monarchy that would conduct elections. She remained the dowager Empress until her death and faced many crises in her forty-seven years of the monarchy. Not least, the assassination of Guangxu by arsenic poisoning. By now, Dowager Cixi was herself ill—in fact, she died only the day after her nephew. Some theories exist that she may have been behind the poisoning because she feared Guangxu would overturn some of her modernisations. However, most authorities believe she was not involved in his death. Whatever, Dowager Empress Cixi led her entire country into an age of development. Because of her resilience, iron will, and shrewd intellect she understood the needs of the time and implemented the actions that were best for her country, her people and the stability of her nation in the face of Western threats.

INDIRA GANDHI (1917–1984)

Indian Stateswoman, Politician, and Former Prime Minister of India. Holds the Title of Being the First and Only Female Prime Minister of India.

Indira Gandhi is famous for being the daughter of one of the founding fathers of modern India, Jawahar Laal Nehru. She is also renowned in her own right for her political achievements. She holds the title of being the first and only female prime minister of India, serving in the role for three long terms. She was later named as one of the "World's 100 Powerful Women Who Defined the Last Century" by *Time* magazine and one of the "Women of the Millennium" by the *BBC*. She is often referred to as the Iron Lady of India. She held a strong relationship with Britain's own Iron Lady, Margaret Thatcher. Indeed, it was Thatcher who advised her regarding one of the biggest crises of her premiership, when in 1984, a group of rebel Sikh separatists seized control of the symbolic Golden Temple in Amritsar. The operation to take back control of the Temple is known as Operation Blue Star and was one of the most controversial events in India's recent history.

Born into the family of Nehru, Indira was bought up in a world of political intrigue. This was a time when India was still a part of the British Empire but was seeking freedom from it. Her father, along with his friend Mahatma Gandhi, was one of the leading figures pushing for independence. She was an intelligent lady who studied at prestigious institutions in India, Switzerland, and England. In 1955, Indira Gandhi joined the Congress political party, and four years later, she was appointed as its president. After her father died in 1964 (he was the prime minister of India at that time—India had gained independence in 1947 in a bloody process known as Partition), she was elected to the upper house of Parliament and named as the minister of information and broadcasting. Her father's successor, Laal Bahadur Shastri, died in 1966, and following his demise, Indira Gandhi was appointed as the first female prime minister of India.

Indira Gandhi is one of the most celebrated figures in India's history. She is regarded as a hero to many, while some depict her as an authoritative leader. She is praised for her common-people-oriented policies and for being there for the underprivileged and the poor. She started the Green Revolution in India to cater to the nutritional requirements of the needy; better seeds and machinery were used to improve yields during harvest. She also sent the first Indian man into space, which is an achievement. India developed politically and economically under her rule and introduced her Five-Year Plans, which led to targeted economic growth. Largely, these were successful. She solidified foreign relations with other countries and made India a strong power in the South-Asian region. Indira even approved the nuclear programme in her nation, making India a stronger global power and gaining international acclaim and recognition.

She died in October 1984, assassinated by her own bodyguards in the aftermath of Operation Blue Star. The treatment of their comrades angered Sikh activists during the operation. The Golden Temple is one of the most important icons in the Sikh religion, and many considered Indira Gandhi to be anti-Sikh in her policies. Her bodyguards were, however, themselves Sikh people. After she was killed, anarchy ruled the streets for a while, with many Sikh people beaten and murdered in vicious uprisings against the actions of those bodyguards. It was a deeply unfortunate end to what was, in most people's eyes, an important and successful period of political progress in India. It cannot be overstated how challenging ruling a country so damaged by centuries of British rule must have been.

Yet Indira Gandhi remains of the most iconic figures in the history of modern India. Because of her powerful will, determination, and her clear picture of what she wanted for her country, she made her mark as one of the longest-serving prime Ministers of India. Despite all the controversy that still centres around her, she largely stabilised India and passed policies that benefited the country in the long run. The global power that India is today is, in significant part, down to her vision.

CHAPTER 5

WOMEN ACHIEVING HEIGHTS OF PRODUCTIVITY AND CREATIVITY

PHILLIS WHEATLEY (1753–1784)

The First African American and Second
Woman to Publish a Book of Poems

Phillis Wheatley spent much of her short life as a slave. She was born in West Africa, most probably the Gambia, and was captured when she was only seven or eight. However, those few years in her homeland stayed with her and were a major influence on the poetry she was soon to write.

If luck is a term which can ever be used for a person who becomes enslaved, then Phillis (her white family named her after the ship on which she travelled from Africa) was more fortunate in this respect than many. The Wheatley family were forward thinking for their time and set about educating the young girl from Africa they bought into their family. Classical languages, astronomy, literature, the bible—within a year, this bright spark was able to read and write herself. She was only fourteen when her first poem appeared in print, and when in 1770, *An Elegiac Poem on the Death of the Celebrated Divine George Whitfield* was published, it caused quite a stir. Not only was it written by a woman, which was moderately unusual in those days, but a woman of colour, one with immediate African heritage and a slave to boot. Unheard of. Literally. News of this remarkable young woman reached the ears of the Countess of Huntingdon across the Atlantic, and she offered financial support for Phillis to travel to England. That she did, the Wheatley's son in tow, and in England, the first book published by an American black woman was born. Titled *Poems on Various Subjects, Religious and Moral*, it caused a considerable amount of interest and earned rave reviews. However, many of Phillis' advocates feared enslavers would claim a black woman was incapable of producing a book of poems, implying that it was written by a white person.

To counter this, a number of well-known Boston intellectuals contributed to the anthology's introduction. Many influences were apparent in the young girl's works. These included religion and the themes made popular by other poets she had studied—most notably Alexander Pope. However, from today's perspective (her works are still popular), it is her elegiac style which is of most note. This reflects her African roots, where it is the role of young girls to sing funeral songs. Something Phillis may well have done while living in her homeland. Such an influence adds poignancy to her poetry and gives it a dimension missing from other writing of the time.

The book encouraged the Wheatleys to give Phillis her freedom, and she became quite political in her outlook. She was a fan of George Washington and an increasingly ardent abolitionist. Yet, the protestant overtones of her writing, the beauty, honesty and intellectual music of her poems won over both abolitionists and many who supported the slave trade alike.

Phillis married a free black man, John Peters, in 1778. Together, they had three children, but none of these survived. Indeed, complications arose while she was in the throes of another childbirth, and Phillis died. Although she continued to write throughout her life, working as a scrub woman to support to enhance their meagre income, her second volume was not published.

Nevertheless, Phillis Wheatley is an icon for black women and first-generation African Americans. It seems obvious today that colour is no barrier to talent, creativity or original thinking. But it took somebody like Phillis to prove the point.

JANE AUSTEN (1775–1817)

One of the Greatest Novelists in English Literature

Jane Austen is, in many people's opinion, the greatest female novelist in the English language. Perhaps the finest irrespective of gender. But even though today her works are synonymous with a drama about the Regency period, and her works are the creative force behind so many Sunday-evening serials and popular films, she was actually little known throughout her lifetime.

Jane was born in a small village in Hampshire and was the daughter of a clergyman, the Rev. George Austen and his wife, Cassandra. She was their second daughter (her sister, and best friend, is also Cassandra) and grew up alongside six brothers. But if money was tight with such a big family, life was good.

When we look at Jane's life, it is not that surprising that she became a novelist. Home was full of books; all the children were encouraged to learn and study—Jane and her sister were sent away to school when they were young—and many an hour was spent scribbling stories and making up plays.

For a woman who wrote about love, Jane's own romantic life was disappointingly brief. During the times in which she lived, parents retained a significant influence on deciding who their children should marry. Her only true love was Tom Lefroy, who, as a man planning a career in law, was considered by his family to be a social step above a country parson's daughter. Since his family sponsored his studies, they felt they had the right to say who he could and could not wed, and unfortunately, 'could not' was the category into which Jane fell. The romance ended, and that was that.

Although Jane did nearly tie the knot, it was to the splendidly-named Harris Bigg-Wither. A proposal for marriage was duly delivered, Jane accepted and almost immediately realised that she did not love Harris. Since, in her novels, her heroines stuck by the principle that love is all, she felt it would be hypocritical to give up her fledgling career for uncertain domestic bliss with somebody toward whom she felt neither attraction nor affection. She withdrew her acceptance of Harris' proposal, and as far as love or marriage were concerned, that was that.

Jane had come so close to making a decision she would probably have regretted the remainder of her life. The world got an even luckier escape. Who knows whether the greatest novels of the Regency period, books right up there with the finest ever penned, would have ever been published had she succumbed to Bigg-Withers' wishes? Imagine a world without *Pride and Prejudice*, *Sense and Sensibility*, *Mansfield Park*, *Emma* or *Northanger Abbey*. Jane's near error may have come about because this period in her life marked one of the few times the family was in turmoil. George had suddenly, unexpectedly announced his retirement. The Austens had therefore been forced to give up their much-loved little cottage in Steventon and had moved to Bath. Then, in 1805, George died, and the family were distraught. Jane, even more than the others, she and her father had been incredibly close.

A time of financial uncertainty followed. Jane had yet to publish her first novel, but it was all hands to the pump and for a short time and writing had to take a back seat. The brothers did what they could to support their mother and sisters, but life was hard.

Then one brother, Edward, rented Chawton Cottage for them. At last, Jane, Cassandra and their mother now had a permanent home that was idyllic enough to enable Jane to return to writing. She did, and other family members took on her domestic responsibilities to allow her to concentrate on her passion. The Austens really were a close-knit group. When a rogue publisher tries to take advantage of Jane—she sees through him and is not conned—another brother, Henry, begins to act as her literary agent. He finds a reliable publisher, and Jane's books reach the world.

She saw her first novel, *Sense and Sensibility*, published in 1811. The novel was a hit and sold out very quickly. She focused on strong female leads who struggled to get social standing and were not shy to voice their opinions on the matter. Austen tried balancing virtue and vice, creating the ideal amalgam to promote good values. *Pride and Prejudice* follows, then *Mansfield Park*. Her readers know they want more but do not know who from. Jane published anonymously—this was not unusual at the time—especially for women. She was extremely modest—for such a great writer, it is an admirable trait, but she also knew that to be named as a woman in the male world of publishing was to find oneself placed at a disadvantage.

Another trait Jane held in abundance was a commitment to hard work. Her novels were meticulously edited and re-written until she found that perfect mix of humour, satire, love and narrative, all told with precision and pace. For a while, life is back to being as good as it was in Steventon. But by April 1817, she is unwell, and she dies that July. Brother Henry now has influence in London, and he can earn his unknown sister a burial place in Winchester Cathedral, just fifteen miles from her childhood home. He also decides it is time for Jane's name to be revealed, and for her to take place as the greatest female writer of all time. A position she still holds today.

HARRIET BEECHER STOWE (1811–1896)

A Renowned American Writer, Philanthropist of Her Time, Inspiring the World Through Her Ideals Depicted in Her Novels

Maybe the most famous anti-slavery novel of all time is Harriet Beecher Stowe's *Uncle Tom's Cabin*. The book makes no bones about the evils of slavery and infuriated many in the American south when it was first published in 1851. It even spawned a generation of copy-cat style books, celebrating slavery as some kind of social good. Unsurprisingly, none of these stories have survived into modern culture. Harriet's book, by contrast, most certainly has.

Harriet was born into a large family, her father being a well-known Congregational minister. Sadly, her mother died when she was just five, and although her father remarried, her elder sister, Catherine, largely brought the young girl up. She enjoyed a fine and liberal education and was exposed to much of the same type of learning as her male peers when she attended the famed Catherine Beecher's Hartford Female Academy and, later, Seminary. As a child and young adult, Harriet's writing stood out. Her future career looked fixed.

At this early stage of her life, she did not have a particular focus on her compositions. She wrote essays, spent a period of time as a teacher and mixed with some of the finest thinkers of her day, people she met through her father's work. She published her first book, *Primary Geography*, in 1833. This was not as it sounds. It was certainly not a school text book. Instead, the book was a celebration of many of the different cultures Harriet had experienced. It was through her father's work as President of the Lane Seminary in Cincinnati that she met Calvin Stowe, who worked as a professor there. The two married, and Calvin was a strong advocate for his wife's writing.

Theirs was a full life, blessed with seven children and challenged by various financial ups and downs. Meanwhile, Harriet's writing remains prolific. She publishes numerous articles in magazines, and produces thirty books, covering everything from novels to religious non-fiction.

But, like so many other people, it takes a tragedy in her life to focus Harriet's mind. Her son dies in a cholera outbreak. She is heartbroken. But this great thinker does not focus solely on her own grief. She understands that the devastation she is feeling is repeated endlessly in the hearts of slaves when their own children are taken from them as her son was. Not through illness, though, but through the actions of their 'owners', who sell the children on for profit.

Harriet's son died in 1849, and the following year, a second event focuses on her mind even more. The Fugitive Act of 1850 is passed. This astonishingly cruel piece of legislation requires people in the North to return any runaway slaves they come across. It is the legislation of political expediency and demonstrates that it is not only in the deep south where the rights of fellow human beings fail to be recognised.

But for Harriet and many abolitionists like her, it is an act of outrage. She writes *Uncle Tom's Cabin, which was* initially serialised in a magazine (often the method through which books first appeared in those days), then it was properly published as a novel in 1852. It is a huge success, selling 300000 copies in that year alone.

Opponents try to deride the novel as the romantic imaginings of an uninformed northerner, a woman at that. Harriet, though, refuses to be riled and instead publishes another work, *Key to Uncle Tom's Cabin*, which includes the sources on which her novel is based.

Harriet had found her calling and spent much of the remainder of her life-giving talks and writing in favour of the abolition of slavery. She left behind a legacy of words which moved an entire cohort of a country to rise against slavery.

CLARA JOSEPHINE SCHUMANN (1819–1896)

"Europe's Queen of the Piano"
A German Classical Musician of the Nineteenth Century

When Clara married Robert Schumann, it was very much in the face of objections from her father. However, it seemed a good partnership since both were highly engaged in the music industry. While Robert's career was defined as a composer, Clara championed the task of performance. After their wedding day, and partly because of an injury to Robert's right hand, she performed many of his works. Clara was an accomplished pianist with the ability to play 'by ear' as well as from scores.

Clara performed in the Leipzig Gewandhaus concert hall when she was just nine and made her formal debut by the age of eleven. Throughout her teenage years, her manager supervised her, who was both strict and supportive. She also wrote her own compositions and played the works of other widely known composers, such as Johann Sebastian Bach, Domenico Scarlatti, Ludwig van Beethoven, and Franz Schubert.

She was also a mother, and a loving and supportive wife. She composed music and toured regularly, juggling these various aspects of her life whilst maintaining her reputation as one of Europe's leading pianists.

Then Robert died. It was a devastating blow and ended Clara's career as a composer. But not as a performer. After his death, she earned the sobriquet Queen of the Piano. Following the passing of her husband, she also devoted a considerable amount of time to editing his work.

Clara truly was a remarkable musician and woman. She left a mark in the music industry as a woman of unmatched resolve, excelling at everything she encountered.

FANNY EATON (1835–1924)

An Inspirational Figure in Victorian Britain Became a Popular Model at London's Royal Academy

While Victorian and Edwardian artists often painted portraits, it was rare indeed that their subjects were black. Fanny Eaton did much to challenge this prejudice. Born the daughter of a freed slave in the English colonies, Fanny moved to London in the 1840s and later became a popular model at London's Royal Academy. She was featured in many prominent paintings by renowned artists of that time, including Dante Gabriel Rossetti, John Everett Millais, and Joanna Mary Boyce.

Although slavery had been banished in Britain by Fanny's day, considerable prejudice still existed. Black people were invisible, and that was a deliberate ploy by society. But Fanny proved to be a paragon of beauty and thus became prominent as a model during the era. She became the subject of art, not an extra in the background, and because of this, contributed to the growing significance of black people in society. Her colour also presented a new challenge to artists of the day, especially the expertise required to capture the pigmentation of her dark-toned skin.

Yet, for all her significance to artists and her role as a pioneer in the world of portraiture modelling, Fanny's influence is still downplayed in Britain. But visit major art museums and we will find pictures that celebrate her individuality.

Although she enjoyed popularity among artists of her day, Fanny still endured the tough life typical of many of her peers. Alongside the inherent prejudice of that era, Fanny lost her husband while young and raised ten children as a single parent. She also never lost her drive to promote the role of black people and to challenge practices and perceptions which were little more than those of slavery times, even if that evil was no longer lawful.

As such, she is an excellent role model for our book. A woman who entered an unusual but public field made an enormous success out of it but never lost touch with her roots or her duties as a mother.

VIRGINIA WOOLF (1882–1941)

British Writer Recognized as One of the Most Innovative Writers of the Twentieth Century

There are few real life people, outside monarchs and presidents, whose names are celebrated in a work of fiction. Virginia Woolf is one of that select little group. Edward Albee's 1960s classic, *Who's Afraid of Virginia Woolf*, becoming a highly successful play of the time, one still frequently revived today. That the play is not about Virginia Woolf (it focuses on the challenges of marriage) is further recognition of her significance as an influencer of her day.

Virginia was born into a somewhat dysfunctional family, and her childhood was notable in contributing to her later life's success as a social writer. She launched a family newspaper, *The Hyde Park Gate News*, where she documented humorous anecdotes from her family. Not that growing up was always that great. Her childhood became abusive because of sexual harassment by her half-brothers, and the sudden death of her mother when she was only thirteen also contributed to her tough upbringing. Virginia was coping with a mental breakdown caused by these twin challenges when, two years later, she also lost her half-sister. She was forced to grow up at a very early age.

However, despite these setbacks, Virginia was academically very successful. She was enrolled in her studies at King's College London, where she became acquainted with several radical feminists, many of whom were working toward educational reform. She began her professional career as a published writer when she contributed to *The Times Literary Supplement* in 1905. In a short time, she became well regarded among literary circles, especially for her novel *Mrs. Dalloway*. The book raised several issues, such as those relating to feminism and homosexuality in post–World War I England, in a mesmerising and often whimsically savage manner. Indeed, her list of novels, which includes *To The Lighthouse*, are considered revolutionary because of their consciousness-raising tone and storyline.

Her distinguished position within literary circles and her revered position in literary society are because of her innovative and influential writing style. Her novels depict the rapid transformations taking place in the world, such as changing gender roles, variations in sexuality, class consciousness, and revolutionising technology.

112

But Virginia Woolf's career did not just embrace the novel. She was a distinguished writer in other respects, producing essays and short stories. She was renowned as a speaker, often taking the floor at universities and expanding young minds. She was also a pioneering feminist and social activist.

Who's afraid of Virginia Woolf? We might well ask. The answer should be nobody whose heart is in the right place.

HATTIE MCDANIEL (1893–1952)

The First African American to Win an Oscar

This talented singer and reciter of poetry was born in Kansas and received her elementary education at a school which was mostly attended by white students. However, racial prejudice was less of an issue where she grew up compared with many other places in the US, and this helped her to showcase her multiple talents at her school. She was an outstanding singer and captivated her audience with her melodious voice. Hattie was also a fine actress. Even during her school days, it was clear where her future career would lie. If the chance was open to her...

Unlike for many African Americans of this time, this proved to be the case. Hattie took her unique capabilities on from performances at school and church and established a professional career, eventually flourishing in the industry. Later, she sang in professional minstrel shows, danced, performed humorous skits, and wrote her own songs.

She also became the first black woman in America to be heard on the radio.

Hattie's career, however, was not all plain sailing. The Great Depression hit, and the arts industry suffered. People simply did not have the money to support it. Like many others, she lost her job as a performer just as she was getting going. But then her hard work and talent earned her a break. Being cast as Aunt Dilsey in the Will Rogers vehicle, *Judge Priest* proved to be a big breakthrough in McDaniel's career. She sang a duet with Rogers, which proved a hit with audiences and the press. Suddenly, Hattie was in demand. She made an astonishing forty films over the next decade while appearing in twelve movies in 1936 alone. It is, though, her performance as Mammy in *Gone with the Wind,* for which she is probably best known. This not only won her an Oscar, she was the first African American woman to be recognised by the Academy, but also meant she achieved financial stability as an actress, earning more than even some of her white contemporaries. A rare feat in any field.

GRETA GARBO (1905–1990)

Swedish American Actress, a Success Story in the World of Hollywood Who Worked Her Way Up with Just Her Talent and Skill

Greta Garbo is a name synonymous with Hollywood's greatest days of the 1920s and 30s. She was a Swedish actress and one of the most glamorous screen stars in Hollywood history. Greta managed that rare feat of being in the centre of the public eye whilst remaining the receiver of their affection and still keeping her privacy. Maybe a part of her charm comes from the fact that despite being one of the world's most famous faces during her heyday, she remained somewhat elusive in real life.

Greta was born into a poor family. Her father was an unskilled labourer who hardly made ends meet. When he became sick, Greta dropped out of school to look after him. She was just thirteen. Sadly, he died two years later from kidney failure. It was then, still as a teen, that Greta vowed she would no longer live a life of poverty and would make a living for herself, of which she could be proud.

She was as good as her word and earned a job as a saleswoman in a Swedish department store. Her role involved some modelling for advertising shorts. Slowly, her name and face began to be noticed, as did her natural instincts in front of the camera. It was these which landed her a role in the European movie *Peter the Tramp* (1922). Ever ambitious, Greta recognised Hollywood as the future of the burgeoning movie industry and moved to America in 1925. She won her first US role in *The Torrent*, in which she played the part of a Spanish peasant who aimed to become an opera star. The movie was an instant hit. Her next two films, *The Temptress* (1926) and *Flesh and the Devil* (1926), were also successful, garnering international praise, and the unknown Swedish girl was suddenly MGM's biggest asset. Greta bargained hard with the moguls in charge of the movie company and won a formidable contract that gave her both autonomy over her roles and a good financial return.

Greta became known for her enigmatic personality and was often referred to as the Spanish Sphinx because of her elusiveness and publicity shunning. Her private life was just that, private, and she earned a reputation as one of the hardest celebrities to interview, which further added to the shroud of mystery surrounding her. Her role in MGM's *Anna Karenina* (1935) was considered the performance of her career, as she brought to life the breathtaking character torn between her two lovers and her son. However, the success of her career was not just down to a pretty face. Greta was a fine and much sought-after actress throughout her movie-making days. But nothing lasts forever. *Two-Faced Woman* (1942) turned out to be a flop and became the final movie of her career. Maybe the war had changed audiences' moods. Greta Garbo never returned to the big screen, living the rest of her life in anonymity. But although her privacy remained, interest in her never diminished.

Later, she was deservedly awarded an honorary Oscar for her brilliant portrayals of women. She was truly a Hollywood success story, starting at the bottom and using her skill and determination to make it to the very top.

ELLA JANE FITZGERALD (1917–1996)

"The Queen of Jazz"
Internationally Acclaimed American Jazz Singer

Ella Fitzgerald proves that a person can overcome a tough childhood and make it big. Of course, it helps if you have the sort of sweet, flexible, caramel flavoured voice with which she was blessed, but determination too characterised this superstar's long career. Whether Ella guessed that one day she would be known as Lady Ella, the Queen of Jazz, and the First Lady of Song, when she was growing up at the Colored Orphan Asylum, is impossible to tell. But if this challenging institution offered anything to a young, black girl on the edges of trouble, it told her she wanted to leave her past behind. Ella Fitzgerald ended up with fourteen Grammy Awards, several other distinctions and international acclaim. She certainly moved on from those tough early years.

She was born the illegitimate child of separated parents, when such a handicap could mark you forever. However, life with her mum was happy, if impoverished. Then her mental and physical health plummeted after her mother's death in 1932. She went to live with an aunt, but it didn't really work out. Her schooling suffered, and soon Ella was getting involved in illegal activities. She was caught by the police and sent to the disturbingly named orphanage above, where she was regularly beaten. Eventually, she escaped this oppressive institution. But even as a youngster, her love for jazz music was always present. Although remarkably given the astonishing voice she held, it was a dance that was her first love. In 1934, she attempted to get herself out of the troubles she was becoming embroiled and attended an amateur night at the Harlem Opera House, where she intended to dance. But at the last minute, she ditched those plans and sang a song instead. The audience was spellbound. They knew that this young girl standing before them could become a superstar. Even though her voice was unpolished, it was dripping with potential and natural talent. Fitzgerald won that amateur night, and the recognition that came with this was what she needed. Suddenly she believed in herself, and her career was underway.

Ella was signed by the Chick Webb Orchestra, who recorded songs with her, many of which became played nationally. Songs like *Rock It for Me* and *I Got a Guy* topped the charts under Webb's name. Later, a song called *A-Tisket, A-Tasket,* was released under Ella's own name. This song—based on a children's poem—also topped the charts and became one of the greatest hits of the decade, earning her enormous popularity and selling almost a million copies. In 1939, Fitzgerald recorded *I Found My Yellow Basket,* a follow-up to *A-Tisket, A-Tasket.* This song also reached the top ten of the charts, making her one of the top-grossing artists of the decade.

When Chick died, the Orchestra took on Ella's name. But she missed her mentor. In 1942, she boldly decided to leave the orchestra and start a solo career. Her first recording as a soloist, *My Heart and I Decided,* reached the top ten of the rhythm and blues (R&B) charts on August 1, 1942. Jazz seems to always remain in fashion, which is undoubtedly partly because of Ella Fitzgerald. Over fifty years after her debut, she made her last recording in 1989, and her last performance was at New York's Carnegie Hall in 1991.

Ella's records always sold like hot cakes. She was one of the top-grossing artists of her time, appreciated both nationally in the US and worldwide. She sold forty million copies of her albums, which remain popular today. In 1987, she was presented with the National Medal of Arts by President Reagan. A few years later, she was honoured as Commander of Arts and Letters by the president of France—proof of her enduring international appeal. Along with these priceless awards, she was presented with honorary doctorates by Ivy League colleges such as Dartmouth and Yale.

Not bad for a girl sent to juvenile custody following the death of her mother.

GWENDOLYN BROOKS (1917–2000)

The First African American to Win a Pulitzer Prize for Literature

Gwendolyn Brooks's subject matter was often focused on the daily struggles facing the urban poor of the black community. In 1949, she published a book of poetry called *Annie Allen*, which observed and celebrated the life of the titular character. It won her the Pulitzer Prize the following year, making Gwendolyn the first African American person to win the award. This was not the only recognition to find its way to her door; she was made poet laureate of Illinois in 1968 and was the first black woman to become a poetry consultant to the library of Congress.

Gwendolyn was born into a working-class and ambitious family. They moved from Kansas to Chicago when Gwendolyn was young, her father working as a janitor but with plans to become a doctor. Her mother, meanwhile, was both a teacher and a classically trained pianist. With such encouragement, it is not surprising that Gwendolyn excelled at school, backed by her parents, and overcame much racism inherent in the Chicago education system of the time.

This attitude of her peers undoubtedly affected her and how she viewed the world. She observed keenly how much the people of the black community had to fight in their daily life to simply keep their heads above water.

After completing her education, Gwendolyn began working as a secretary to make ends meet, but writing remained her passion. She joined a workshop targeted at helping writers and poets, supervised by Inez Cunningham Stark, a strong woman with a literary background. Inez guided Gwendolyn and helped her polish her raw style. But without modifying it too much. Gwendolyn's willingness to experiment with style and form helped her gain international recognition for her works and become one of the leading American poets of her day.

She had published her first anthology, *A Street in Bronzeville*, in 1943, which found much success, especially considering that poetry inhabits a small niche in the world of publishing. People admired Brooks's writing style along with what she wrote. Following *Annie Allen*, she published her first and only novel, *Maud Martha*, which also employed an interesting form. Written as a series of vignettes, the novel examines the prejudices suffered by the eponymous Maud. The discrimination she faces not only comes from the white community but also from fairer-skinned African Americans. The book contains autobiographical elements in this respect.

Brooks was no ordinary poet; she felt the anguish of people and communicated that through her words. As she became older, she focused more on the civil rights movement, offering an original and incisive insight into the struggles faced by the black community. Perhaps her greatest strength, or certainly the element of her writing, which separates her from many of her peers, was the absence of bitterness in her works. She had that rare ability to show the bitter feelings of her subjects without employing that emotion herself.

ANNE FRANK (1929–1945)

Made a Mark on the World After Writing a Diary
Whilst in Hiding from the Nazis in Amsterdam

Is there a sadder, more tragic true story in literature than that of Anne Frank? Her name is synonymous with the evils of Naziism, the tragedy of war, the cruelty of humanity, but also the optimism inherent in our species. Born into a German Jewish family, Anne's tranquil, happy life turned upside down because of the racism of Nazi German.

Ironically, Anne's father, Otto, had been a lieutenant in the German army. Then he became a businessman, expanding his interests in Germany and outward into the Netherlands. However, Hitler's rise to power made the family realise that it was not safe to stay in Germany because of the growing hostility toward Jews that was becoming prevalent there.

This threat caused the Frank family to move to the Netherlands in 1933. After spending a decade living a normal and relatively comfortable life, the 1940s saw a turning point in the fate of the Frank family and others like them. Fearing capture, Anne and her family moved into a secret flat at the top of a tall, narrow house in Amsterdam. They relied on the care of a local Dutch woman and friend of the family,

Miep Gies, who provided food for them and kept them informed of developments in the war. But the small, secret annexe in which they lived was barely big enough for one family. Into it were squeezed two, along with a difficult older Jewish man. Liberation was in sight when the Germans received a tip off and raided the house. They captured Anne, her family, and the others who lived in the house. The family had evaded detection for over two years, but now they faced the concentration camps. As for Miep, it was likely she would have been shot had it not been that both she and the police officer who interviewed her were from Vienna. The officer covered up what she had done, or perhaps he secretly admired her bravery or despised the Nazis. History does not tell us. Miep returned to the house and removed the Frank's and the other family's papers and meagre possessions in the forlorn hope that she might one day be able to return them. Among this collection was a diary. It belonged to Anne, and Miep vowed not to read it out of respect for the young girl.

The concentration camps were, in reality death camps. Although both Anne and her sister survived for a while, they caught typhus, and both died. Again, they just missed out on liberation. Otto was the only survivor of the eight people who lived squeezed into that tiny flat.

When Anne was gifted her diary on her thirteenth birthday, it first became a place to write accounts about the school, her friends and her innermost thoughts. Soon it would become the most famous record of the life for the Jewish victims of Nazi Germany.

Anne was only fifteen at the time of her death, but her diary recorded the challenges, joys and hopes of daily life for a young girl moving toward adulthood. In writing about herself, her family, and the other people in hiding, Anne offered a permanent record and a clear account of life for Jewish victims of the Nazis. She had planned to publish a book about her time in hiding after the war, and her dream came true. What she could not have imagined, though, is that she would become perhaps the most famous teenage girl in the world's history. Even today, thousands of people fascinated and saddened by the life she lived visiting the annexe where she stayed daily.

Miep, too, achieved her goal. She found Otto after the war, and gave him the papers—including Anne's still unopened diary. Who can imagine the agony and joy he must have felt in reading those simple words his daughter had recorded? Otto swore to publish the journal, to ensure Anne's dream and her account both became reality. He, too could not have imagined the impact they would have. Otto lived until 1980. Let's hope the family is once more together, even now.

Although she did not live long, Anne's legacy continues to reign in the hearts of people. Her diary is a key document in the annals of war literature. More than this, it is the story of a real person and plays its part in ensuring the wickedness of Naziism will never be allowed to rule again.

MIRIAM MAKEBA (1932–2008)

"Mama Africa"
Inspirational South African Singer and
Forthright Opponent of Apartheid

Miriam Makeba, Mama Africa, died as she would have wished, performing in front of her thousands of fans. She had just participated in a concert and suffered a heart attack backstage. At that moment, the anti-apartheid movement of South Africa lost one of its most passionate and effective advocates. Although fortunately, her work was by then largely done. Certainly, inequality still existed in South Africa in 2008, but thanks to Miriam and her peers, the worst was over.

Miriam was an internationally acclaimed singer who performed globally and with stars such as Paul Simon during his various *Graceland* tours. She furthered her music career by singing with the anti-apartheid movement. She was the first black musician to leave South Africa because of apartheid, and many others followed her over the years.

Miriam's early life, however, was tough. As a child, her family lived in considerable poverty, and Miriam worked as a household cleaner in order to contribute to family income. However, she soon realised the magic inherent in music, although she could not have known that her astonishing voice would see her be able to throw off the shackles of poverty. Though her musical abilities were praised at a very early age, Miriam was black, and that meant she lacked any strong support behind her. However, she was relentless in her ambition and continued her struggle until she was old enough for her music career to progress enough to offer her some independence. She began singing within a local township group before gaining her global reputation for her voice and her politics.

Miriam's musical breakthrough arrived when she joined the Manhattan Brothers, a top band of that era. She sang alongside Abigail Kubeka, Mummy Girl Nketle, and Mary Rabatobi as a part of a female group called the Sunbeams. However, during her life in South Africa,

Miriam suffered the injustice of the apartheid system, which she recalled in her autobiography.

But hard work, belief and determination can overcome many obstacles. Miriam had time to take part in a global tour with the Manhattan Brothers. She garnered a reputation and was allowed to perform as a solo artist during an eighteen-month tour of Africa. This was after the African Jazz and Variety Review recruited her. Her reputation was enhanced this time even among the more liberal aspects of the white community after she received rave reviews playing the female lead in *King Kong*. Miriam continued to advance her career. She appeared at the 1959 Venice Film Festival, performing a vocalist role in a documentary on black life called *Come Back, Africa*. From there, she was taken to London, where she spoke on television and played at the Village Vanguard jazz club.

The white minority who ran South Africa liked neither Miriam's politics nor her success. She was exiled from her homeland. But this did not hold Miriam back in her goal of enlightening the world about the horrors of apartheid, a system the 'liberal west' ignored. She appeared at the UN Special Committee Against Apartheid, there to speak against the atrocities of this discriminatory and violent system. The South African government responded by banning her records. Miriam continued to fight for her cause, taking part in events that fought not only against the apartheid system but also for the civil rights movement. White racists like little less than a powerful, popular, successful black woman. She was exiled from many other countries sympathetic to South Africa's system. They could banish her, but they could not keep Miriam down. She was able to recruit a pan-African ensemble of musicians to spread her word globally, including in South Africa. Thus, despite the limitations placed on her freedoms, Miriam was able to apply her ideas on black consciousness to all corners of the world.

Even today, her life remains a powerful legacy to inspire people to fight for global justice.

CHAPTER 6

WOMEN'S CONTRIBUTIONS IN WAR AND MILITARY SERVICE

BOUDICCA (30–61)

Fearless "Warrior Queen"
Queen of the Celtic Iceni Tribe

Boudicca is a woman so great they named her five times. She is also known as Boudica and Boadicea, the Warrior Queen and the Queen of Revolt, being a queen who revolted for the good of her wronged people. Her uprising against the conquering army of Romans saw her recorded in history as a symbol of bravery and resistance. Britain's history is full of people who drove out invaders, but the name of this fearless queen stands up there with the best of them.

Boudicca ruled the Iceni tribe in Southern England with her husband, King Prasutagus. Their kingdom had been forced into a kind of coalition with the Romans. In return for peace, Prasutagus agreed to name the heir of the Romans as the co heir to his throne as well. When Prasutagus died in 60 AD without leaving behind a male heir, the Romans plundered and confiscated the Iceni's lands and wealth. If taking away whatever they possessed was not enough, the Roman governor in Iceni, Gaius Suetonius Paulinus, had Boudicca publicly flogged and her daughters raped by Roman soldiers.

This stoked the fire of vengeance inside Boudicca, who then gathered all her forces and tribes to rebel. Like all Celtic women of the time, Boudicca had been honed into a warrior right from childhood. She had been trained for battle. With her massive army of troops, she bit away at the Romans continuously, often razing their cities to the ground. She wanted revenge, and she was getting it.

To show the scale of her aggression, historians estimate that Boudicca and her army killed upwards of seventy thousand Romans in their attacks. But the Romans were nothing if not militarily skilled. Where there is glory, a fall often soon follows. Boudicca and her forces were defeated in the brutal Battle of Watling Street. The Romans, led by their governor Gaius Suetonius Paulinus, carefully manipulated the ground for this battle. The Romans launched a pincer movement, attacking from both front and back, eventually killing everyone in Boudicca's insurgent army.

Boudicca refused to be captured. She consumed poison before the Romans could catch her and carry out whatever vengeance they planned.

She may have ultimately been defeated, but Boudicca will always be remembered as the queen with fire in her veins and rebellion in her spirit. Her story is often recounted as the Rise of the Fallen Queen. Today, she is still admired for her daunting bravery and fearless actions, for being a true queen who fought for the rights of her people in the face of an overwhelmingly powerful foe.

JOAN OF ARC (1412–1431)

A Patriot Warrior and Heroine of France

Joan of Arc, also known as the Maid of Orleans, was a young peasant girl who rose to lead the French Army to the embattled city of Orleans. It is believed that she was only nineteen when she died, burned at the stake, but already this young heroine had achieved several great military victories. In gaining these victories, she had installed Charles VII as the right and proper King of her nation, ousting the English monarch, Henry VI, who had inherited the throne after his father stole it from the French during the 100-years-war.

Joan of Arc was the chosen one. At least in the perception of her followers and herself. Although, this was not immediately apparent. She was raised as a peasant girl and trained to care for animals. She was also a skilled seamstress, but it was not these talents which marked her out to go down in history. Her mother was a devout Catholic and instilled a deep love of the Church in her daughter. At 13, the young girl experienced divine visions that became so persistent and vivid that she realised God had chosen her to free her nation from the shackles imposed by the English. To do this, she must lead the French Army in their long-lasting war with their unfriendly neighbours. Quite how a girl with such humble beginnings gained so senior a position is hard to say. It appears she met her prince in exile, Charles, and persuaded him to allow her to lead a force from his army. So convinced was he by the girl's passion and her belief that she held divine guidance that he agreed to her request, albeit against much opposition from his court.

By this time, Joan had followers of her own. French folklore states that a virgin will lead it from trouble, and many held that Joan was this virgin. Dressed in white armour, riding a white horse, she headed to Orleans, where the English, backed by turncoat French aristocracy from Burgundy, held the city in a long and bitter siege.

She attacked many times, each relieving the English grip just a little, until the hated enemy eventually fled. Victorious, Joan led her prince to Reims, where he was invested in the throne. Emboldened, Joan—supported by Charles—led further attacks. She planned to even retake Paris, but the men at court were wary. Joan was young, a peasant, and most important of all, a woman. She might cut her hair short and dress like a man, but it hurt their dignity and their pride to allow a woman to achieve what they could not.

Instead, Charles VII sent her to relieve the city of Compiegne, where Burgundian forces had taken hold. Here, she was thrown from her horse and captured. The French traitors took her to the nearest English stronghold, where she was imprisoned and tortured and charged with seventy offences, from dressing as a man to being a witch.

Suddenly, Charles VII, for so long her supporter, and the man who owed his throne to this brave young girl, lost interest. His ear battered by the constant criticism of Joan, especially from his right-hand man, Georges de la Trémoille, he abandoned her, apparently taking heed of the English claims that Joan was a heretic.

Eventually, after holding out for a year, she signed a confession, then immediately withdrew it. This was the sign the English needed, and she was burnt at the stake. Thus, the Patron Saint of France was born, and the greatest martyr in the nation's history created.

Indeed, death was only the starting point for Joan. A posthumous trial was held for the martyred heroine, and her name was cleared. Over the next half a millennium, she acquired increasingly mythical status, and in 1909 she was beatified in Notre Dame Cathedral. Eleven years later, she was made a saint.

JACQUELINE COCHRAN (1906–1980)

An American Wartime Leader and Pilot
Who Broke Numerous Records

Jacqueline Cochran broke aviation records with more regularity than glasses are smashed in a buy city centre pub on a Saturday night. She was one of the most incredible pilots in US history and set eight records for speed, altitude, and distance. Her achievements were both national and global. She was an unstoppable girl, the fastest flyer of her time and the first-ever woman to break the sound barrier.

Jacqueline's upbringing was unusual, to say the least. She was raised in DeFuniak Springs, Florida, but liked to pretend she was an orphan. She wasn't but had decided at an early age to leave home. An independent girl, she didn't want anyone to interfere in her personal matters. She had a wild streak in her but was also persistent in her determination to achieve her goals. By just ten years of age, she was working in the cotton industry but soon left it to join a beauty salon. Being a multi-talented woman, she also studied nursing. Jacqueline enjoyed her long period of working as a beautician. She was ambitious and performed all her duties with utter enthusiasm. She garnered a fine reputation in the industry and worked her way up to the fashionable Antoine's salons in Saks Fifth Avenue stores in New York City and Miami.

Floyd Odlum, her future husband, saw the determination and courage which flooded the personality of this young lady. He encouraged her to learn to fly. Maybe it wasn't surprising that she took to this new skill with the ease of a bird in the sky. Her speed was unmatchable. She achieved altitudes unheard of and could cover great distances in a single bound. It appeared that every time she got into an aircraft, everyone waited for her to achieve her latest record.

Then, with Jacqueline's career at its peak, war broke out in Europe. Like many other women and fellow pilots, she had a firm belief that the skills of women should be utilised in the war effort to help defeat the Axis powers. When Jacqueline spoke, people listened. Even the hawks in the US air force. In 1941, with the war threatening to end the wrong way, she selected a group of twenty-seven highly qualified and skilled US women pilots to ferry military aircraft in Great Britain for the Air Transport Auxiliary (ATA).

Jacqueline might not be as well-known as some women in this book, but she truly was a hero, an innovator and a perfect inspiration and role model for women and girls of today.

IRENA SENDLER (1910–2008)

Incredible Polish Woman Who Rescued 2,500 Jewish Children in World War II

Oscar Schindler was a hero and a saviour of the second world war, rescuing hundreds of Jewish people from the gas chamber. He was rightly remembered in the Spielberg film Schindler's list. But others did their bit to help the Jews. We have already seen Miep Gies, who did much to save the Frank family. Another unsung hero is Irena

Sendler, a Polish woman whose bravery and ingenuity rescued thousands of Jewish children.

As director of the children's department for the Council of Aid to Jews, she acted as a part of the resistance groups seeking to preserve the lives of Jewish citizens as Hitler's Nazis sought to imprison them and murder them in death camps.

She was born in Warsaw, the daughter of a doctor and his wife, and early on, they moved to the smaller city of Otwock. The concept of sacrifice hit home early for Irena; an outbreak of typhus hit the region when she was just seven, and her father died after contracting the disease and treating patients. 'I was taught that if you see a person drowning, you must jump into the water to save them, whether you can swim or not', she said, as a tribute to her father.

She was a bright girl and advanced to university. However, discrimination was rife in Europe as world war two approached, and she vandalised her grade card in protest at the ghetto bench system, a form of segregation growing among certain universities. That got her suspended for three years. It also marked the beginning of her remarkable career as a humanitarian.

Irena was an incredibly resourceful woman. She began assisting Jews in Warsaw as soon as the Germans invaded, but a ghetto was built, and that meant she could not access those in trouble. This was in 1940, and she at once began using her position as a social worker to help. She had a friend who worked at the Contagious Disease centre and got papers from this colleague (they were both a part of the underground resistance group, Zegota) to allow her access to the ghetto. Once there, she set about smuggling children away from this compound. It is believed she and her team saved at least two and a half thousand young lives.

Her work was astonishingly dangerous, and somehow the authorities got wind of her actions. She was arrested and tortured to get her to reveal details of other members of Zegota. But Irena's resourcefulness once more came through. She fed her captors false information, which they absorbed. Next, she was sentenced to death, but her resistance groups bribed the staff at her prison, and she escaped.

In a somewhat pathetic attempt to save face, the Nazis spread the fake news that they had shot Irena. But the heroine stayed in hiding, and once the war was over, set about reuniting the children she had smuggled to orphanages and sanctuaries with their parents. It was a thankless and dispiriting task. The Nazis had killed most of those parents. Irena received many awards in recognition of her bravery, including a nomination for the Nobel Peace Prize, the prestigious Order of the White Eagle from her home nation and the rare and highly special Righteous Among the Nations award.

With a wonderful element of irony, Irena spent her last years cared for by a woman called Elzbieta Ficowska. Without Irena, Elzbieta would not have been alive to perform her good deed. Elzbieta was one of the young children Irena had saved from the death camps.

Although the rest of the world does not agree, Irena never considered herself a heroine. Instead, with typical modesty, she said that she regretted not doing more. A remarkable woman.

NOOR INAYAT KHAN (1914–1944)

A Brave and Successful Allied Spy of Indian Heritage

One of the highest awards for bravery is the George Cross. Since its inception, it has been awarded only twelve times to women. One of these awards was made to Noor Inayat Khan, a British spy who displayed astonishing courage after her capture by the Nazis.

Noor was directly descended from Indian Muslim royalty. She had been born in Moscow, the daughter of an Indian father and mother who was American. She spent a much-travelled childhood—she was a shy, quiet girl but self-sufficient—taking in first London and then Paris, where she was living when the city fell in November 1940. Noor escaped to England and joined the WAAF, the Women's Auxiliary Air Force. Two years later, she joined the Special Operations Executive––Britain's spy department—as a radio operative. In 1943 she was given the codename Madelaine and was secreted into Paris to support the 'Prosper' resistance group. But almost as soon as she arrived, the network was broken, and many of the activists were arrested. Noor could have made her way back into Britain but remained in France, sending as much information back to London as she could manage. What made her bravery even more remarkable was that Noor suffered from a foot condition which made movement tough for her. Indeed, it had led some of her spymasters to question whether she was up to the job. Evidently, their concerns were misplaced.

But life for a spy in occupied France was incredibly dangerous, with threats where they are least expected. Noor's capture came about not through any fault of her own but thanks to betrayal by a French woman. Unfortunately, she was captured with records of her secret signals, which the Germans used to trick other spies into danger.

However, Noor more than made up for this unfortunate occurrence by refusing to speak to her investigators. She even escaped the Gestapo but was caught, put in chains, left in solitary confinement and tortured. Still, she refused to speak. The Gestapo decided that enough was enough and sent Noor (along with three other lady spies they had captured) to a concentration camp, where they shot them all.

It was for this courage in keeping her silence and so saving many more lives that this heroine of the war was awarded the George Cross posthumously, in 1949.

NANCY HARKNESS LOVE (1914–1976)

American Pilot and Commander During World War II
Who Headed the First Group of Women Pilots to Fly
for the US Military

Among the many outstanding and hardworking women whose heroics helped the Allies to win the second world war, Nancy Harkness Love is a prominent figure who carved her place into the history of the

United States. Besides being an American pilot and commander during World War II, she inspired the women of her country and laid the pathways toward equality and opportunity.

Nancy was born into a socially active family in which her father, Robert, was a famous and well-to-do physician. Her parents were determined to ensure that their children received the best education they could, one in which Nancy and her brother could take the opportunity to opt for the field of their interest. For Nancy, that was aviation. Planes transfixed her. But her parents disapproved; they decided that aviation was not an appropriate career for women. But the persistent Nancy convinced her parents that she could break through this glass ceiling and ultimately trained as a pilot. She would fly higher and higher until she roamed in the clouds, and her love for flying grew stronger and deeper. She received her official pilot's licence at nineteen, a remarkable feat.

Nancy was fearless. And wild. She was an adventurous woman, but also one who used her intellect to problem solve. Being an intrepid barnstorming pilot, she soon headed up the first group of women pilots to fly for the US military. Brave, skilled, intelligent and deeply patriotic: she became one of the finest pilots in US history.

It is not surprising that, despite her skills, Nancy experienced misogynism from her male colleagues, especially those in charge. But she stuck to her view that women could contribute to the war effort. They just needed to be given a chance.

Nancy became the pride of the United States. She became a symbol of patriotism and courage and assisted the US military using her skills and competency to lead her team and help the US to gain mastery of the skies. She logged over 1,200 flight hours in 1942 alone, allowing her to become a queen of the air.

SUSAN AHN CUDDY (1915–2015)

First Female Korean Gunnery Officer, Who Took Part in Freeing Korea from Japanese Colonialism

Susan Ahn Cuddy was born in the United States, but her family were Korean activists seeking to liberate their homeland from Japanese colonialism. Indeed, her father died fighting for his beliefs. The legacy he passed to Susan was one of duty and patriotism, leading her to become the first female Korean gunnery officer.

But Sarah faced many obstacles in her life, even in the US, where prejudice existed against her culture and her race. This created many hurdles in her private and professional life. But it was nothing compared to the cruel conditions Japanese colonialism created in Korea. This was a point of concern for Susan and her family.

Then World War II broke out, and Susan signed up, determined to play her part in freeing Korea from ferocious Japanese rule. Or at least tried to sign up. The US authorities deemed neither her race nor her Asian heritage appropriate and refused her application. Susan, though, was determined. And committed. And refused to accept the authorities' decision. She applied again and was given a place in the WAVES (the women's section of the US Naval Reserve).

What followed was a miraculous journey in the United States Navy. Ultimately, it earned her an award from the US government. Every new venture was tackled with commitment, passion, and determination. She became a link trainer, and a gunnery officer, and worked with US Navy Intelligence, the Library of Congress, and the National Security Agency in Washington DC. She was promoted to the rank of lieutenant because of her endeavours. Like others of her gender, she became a symbol of bravery and patriotism.

Sarah is now a role model for all modern army officers, whether male or female. Her impressive chain of accomplishments and victories has stood the test of time. During the cold war, she was appointed to lead a section of over three hundred people who worked in the Russian centre. Her genius and stalwart personality made her a popular and successful leader. The government recognised her work, and, in 1956, she received a fellowship from the National Security Agency to study at the University of Southern California. During her long career, she also worked with the Department of Defense and other agencies on many important projects for the welfare of the country.

The iconic Susan Ahn Cuddy also helped to free Korea from Japanese colonialism and spent decades of her life serving the US Navy. In recognition of her public service and lifetime commitment, the State Assembly of California of District 28 awarded her the Woman of the Year award in 2003.

LILIAN BADER (1918–2015)

First Black Woman to Join the British Armed Forces

The colour of one's skin should never be a barrier to anything. But sadly, too often in the past, it was. Even more shamefully, racial discrimination is still a problem today. Lilian Bader was determined not to let it stand in front of her ambitions, and she is celebrated as the first black woman to join the British armed forces. Both her colour and her father's West Indian heritage were perceived as barriers to her progress by those in charge and indeed forced her to leave her job at the Navy Army Air Force Institute (NAAFI), but Lilian was resolute in achieving her goals regardless of the racially motivated problems she faced.

Many young black women during Lilian's day found themselves in domestic service, and she was no different. But at twenty, she joined the NAAFI. Albeit as a canteen assistant. However, discrimination was rife and forced Lilian out of her job. Her family had enjoyed careers in the armed services, and she was determined to follow in their footsteps.

Once more, it was the outbreak of World War II which opened up opportunities for women like Lilian. Such was the need for volunteers to join that even black women were given their chance. Lilian seized the opportunity and enlisted successfully in the Royal Air Force (RAF). The Women's Auxiliary Air Force accepted her in 1941, where she was the only black person among the white recruits. Being a black woman may have made her something of an anomaly, and no doubt some of her peers treated her poorly (while others were more open-minded), but she was a talented woman and soon became a leading aircraftwoman and an instrument repairer at the RAF. By 1944, she had earned the rank of acting corporal thanks to her positivity and determination. Such promotion may not seem much. But for a black woman to be placed in charge of white recruits was unusual for the time.

Lilian left the army to raise her family but was keen to share the experiences and challenges of being a black woman in a white woman's world. Journalists, politicians, and television shows took a keen interest in knowing about her experience facing racism during her time in the British Armed Forces. Her legacy as the first black woman to join them is still relevant today. Her stories of discrimination, even (and maybe especially) at the highest levels of the Forces, carry weight even in current times. It is sad to report. However, that a woman, especially a black one, should live through this, and overcome such discrimination, is uplifting and offers optimism for the future.

JANE KENDEIGH (1922–1987)

American Navy Flight Nurse Who Was the First Lady Nurse to Appear on an Active Pacific Battlefield

Jane Kendeigh deserves her place among the greatest humanitarians in world history. She was the first Navy flight nurse in the US. Not only did this mark her name for posterity, but many subsequent Navy flight nurses regarded Jane as a distinctive role model.

Jane was an exceptional child. Her dream was always to become a nurse. She realised that dream when she graduated from the prestigious nursing school in Cleveland. It is easy to see how the profession attracted her; as a young person determined to dedicate herself to humanity, it made sense that she opted for a career that enabled her to fulfil her goals.

Jane enjoyed an influential and prolonged time working as a US Navy nurse. As remarkable as it might seem, given the challenges of her environment, she found joy in saving lives, in helping victims back to health. During World War II, she believed her skills could be utilised on the front line. The welfare of her country came above any personal considerations. She was just twenty-two years old when she was posted to help evacuate the injured from the battlefield to the hospital. Jane, along with other nurses, evacuated no less than 2,393 marines and sailors. As well as being the first female nurse on a Pacific battlefield, her dynamism and sharp thinking made her one of the biggest assets and most valuable of women in US wartime history.

Nursing is a profession requiring dedication, humility and skill in which incredible people work tirelessly to bring relief to their patients. Jane was one of the most wonderful and enthusiastic nurses in any nation, and her efforts have set her up as a role model to inspire nurses across the entire world. The nursing community pays her absolute respect. She continued working in her profession after the war, bringing relief to so many more patients. Every crisis, whether in war or peace, is a frightening challenge for the sufferer, whenever and wherever it occurs. Jane, and so many like her, was there to help. Her life, being an embodiment of selflessness and humanity, is a paragon for all modern women striving on their own path to success.

CHAPTER 7

WOMEN WITH WANDERLUST AND CONSERVATIONISTS

GUDRID THORBJARNARDÓTTIR (980–1019)

Most Travelled Woman of the Middle Ages

Challenges in childhood can trigger goals to which people aspire. Whether a young Gudrid Thorbjarnardóttir really planned to be the first non-native woman to give birth on the immense and, so history would have us believe, an undiscovered continent of North America might push imaginations a little far. But that she was a remarkable explorer seems pretty much beyond doubt.

Iceland can be a challenging place to eke out a living, with even subsistence farming being an uncertain way of life. So when Gudrid's father could not provide for the family, they moved to Greenland. While such a journey might end up in a land even more unforgiving than the rocky outcrop that is Iceland, it set within Gudrid a wanderlust which would see her become the greatest female traveller of the ages. We don't know much about Gudrid's life, with records limited to two contemporary sagas, *The Saga of Erik the Red* and *The Saga of the Greenlanders*. However, it appears Gudrid, married in Greenland, was widowed, then married again. Her second husband also had itchy feet, and when a large contingent of these brave Vikings set off for a land across the ocean, Gudrid and her partner were there on board.

Records show they landed on the tip of what we know today as Newfoundland. The sagas refer to Vinland, which is the Viking name for America, and many artefacts have been found in the remains of the settlements. A Viking spinning machine shows women were present, and it looks as though the settlement was occupied for three years.

Therefore, the evidence is strong that the sagas are accurate, and Gudrid was indeed one of the first visitors to set foot on the great continent. That her son was born there marks her out as particularly special.

Historical accounts suggest that Thorbjarnardóttir's journey to North America preceded Christopher Columbus by almost five hundred years, whose own discovery of the new land occurred at the end of the fifteenth century.

Gudrid's travels were far from over. From America, she crossed the Atlantic the other way, settled in Norway, revisited Greenland, and eventually ended up back where it all began, in Iceland. There she converted to Christianity and embarked on a pilgrimage to Rome. Back in Iceland, she ran a farm, like her father.

History tells us that the Vikings, with their longboats, were great travellers. It also confirms that, although they were great and fearsome warriors, this part of their culture is somewhat over-exaggerated. Instead, they would travel as great communities, taking wives, children and artefacts with them. Still, to travel to the extent of Gudrid is unreported elsewhere, making her a truly remarkable woman of her age.

JEANNE BARET (1740–1807)

The First Woman to Circumnavigate the World

Travelling across the world as anything other than a passive tourist or emigrant was frowned upon in the eighteenth century. Extensive travel for work was largely considered the realm of men, so much so that when Jeanne Baret formed part of the French team circumnavigating the world from 1766 to 1769, she dressed as a man and adopted the name Jean. Such was the gender prejudice against women.

Jeanne was a serious scientist who specialised in flora. Her interest in plants had been embedded during her childhood and was tended to and watered by her family. Indeed, her fascination was so great that she was known as the "herb woman." During the great, three-year voyage, she assisted her husband, Dr. Philibert Commercon, in assembling an enormous collection of natural history specimens. She used her knowledge and talent to gather plant samples now showcased in the Paris Natural History museum. Like many women, especially in the fields of science and exploration, her name is undersold and rarely appears among the collection, with credit for discoveries usually awarded to men. Her interest in botany was recognised and acknowledged in the book by Denis Diderot, *Supplement to the Bougainville Voyage*. Later, the French Naval Service, which awarded her a pension for her services, also celebrated her accomplishment.

Little, though, is otherwise known about Jeanne's life. An image, although the only one of its kind, appears of her. Here she is about to embark on her expedition with the French Navy disguised as a man. She is the only female participant, and the images present her as a revolutionary icon, symbolising her as a figure of liberty. Baret's image shows her in loose clothes, which cloak her breasts, which are further bound with linen bandages. She wears a red cap, and a bunch of flowers represent her interest in botany.

Thus, Jeanne became a symbol of French liberty, having the courage to challenge the prevailing norms of that time. This brave and pioneering woman represented the struggle for liberty and freedom which was growing in France.

LOUISE ARNER BOYD (1887–1972)

First Woman to Lead an Arctic Expedition

Born into a wealthy family whose money came from the mid-nineteenth century California Gold Rush, Louise Arner Boyd's parents died when she was young. They left their fortune to their only daughter. Her father had established the Boyd Investment Company in San Francisco, and on his death, Louise became President of the successful business. However, she had been born with the spirit of wanderlust and used her incredible wealth to embark on the journey, which would see her become the first woman to lead an Arctic expedition.

In fact, between 1926 and 1941, she sponsored several expeditions to the ice-covered northern reaches of the world, and it was on one of these that she seized the opportunity to head up the adventure. Her expedition was especially significant thanks to her talent for photography and filmmaking. These skills enabled her to record previously unphotographed regions of the Arctic, such as in Greenland. Her pictures captured the incredible topography of the land, the sea ice, glacial features and land formations of this remarkable kingdom. She also measured ocean depths and captured plant specimens. She further made use of a new technology, an aerial mapping camera, to get pictures of the glacial landscape. Later, these images served in the formation of detailed maps of the region. Her precise, high-quality pictures even proved crucial for early researchers in climate change, providing them with critical information on glacial land transformation and thus enabling them to analyse the changes taking place in the environment.

Louise's distinctive style and creativity while leading the Arctic expedition was acknowledged across the globe. As the first woman to explore the Arctic, she earned several honours, such as election to the council of the American Geographical Society. The scientific community made use of Boyd's talents and skills to achieve its own advancement in the fields of geography and environmental studies. Certainly, Louise was born with the good fortune of considerable wealth. Where she stands out from other vastly rich people is that she ensured her money was employed for the good of mankind. To further its knowledge of the world.

LADY GRACE HAY DRUMMOND-HAY (1895–1946)

The First Woman to Travel the World in a Zeppelin

Little in the early life of the impressively named Lady Grace Hay Drummond-Hay showed she would become such a famed and intrepid traveller. Born in Liverpool, in a gentrified part of Toxteth, her father was the managing director of an animal food company. Her aunt was a well-known dancer; her father's business supplied food, hunting dogs and game rather than your common or garden mutt. Hers was a family with aspirations. It seems she enjoyed a suitably middle class education, and then Grace married Sir Robert Hay Drummond-Hay, a diplomat fifty years her senior. However, he died in 1926 after just six years of marriage, and Grace filled the gap in her life through travel as a global correspondent. She worked on papers in Britain and the United States throughout her career.

It was the fact that she was a journalist that landed Lady Grace Hay Drummond-Hay her spot as the first woman to travel the world in a Zeppelin. It was 1928 when she took off under the giant gas-filled ship, and that was for the transatlantic journey from Germany to America. Five other reporters accompanied her, Grace being the only woman among them. This earned her an enormous amount of attention in the global press. She was writing for Hearst Newspapers, and when, the following year, the Graf Zeppelin embarked on a worldwide journey, it made sense that Grace was there on board to tell the story. She was again the only woman among the 60 passengers and crew.

Her informative stories fuelled a Western enthusiasm for this kind of global travel, especially in America. Later, she reported on the horrors of the war in Ethiopia. She also served as a foreign correspondent in Manchuria, China.

Grace was an intrepid woman of her era. Wealthy and privileged, yet one who once more used the advantages of her life to educating others, at the same time gaining experiences that no other woman had faced.

ALOHA WANDERWELL (1906–1996)

"The World's Most Widely Travelled Girl"
Canadian American Explorer who Pursued Her
Goals and Achieved the Unthinkable

It is unlikely there has ever been a better named traveller than Aloha Wanderwell. Sadly, it is not her birth name. Aloha was born Idris Galcia Welsh and changed her name to Hall when her mother remarried. While it was later in life that she became famous, Aloha dreamt of travelling right from being a child. Her father had written a collection of books containing exciting tales of his own travels, and this inspired her own ambitions.

She was, though, a determined child. A tomboy tall for a woman—as an adult, she stood six feet high in her socks—who had a rebellious streak. Her teachers found her difficult, because she was a girl who refused to be constrained by the limitations of school and textbooks. Maybe a part of the problem was that during her education, Aloha was a fish out of water. The family had travelled to Europe to be with Aloha's stepfather, but he was killed at Ypres in the First World War. She was sent to various European boarding schools, places not renowned for the inspiration of their teaching. For Aloha, there was a vastly exciting world out there, and she wanted to explore it. Something which, as an adult, she certainly did.

Aloha was only sixteen when she set out on a world expedition, which was led by her future husband, Captain Wanderwell. He had adopted the name and was participating in a global race featuring Model T

Fords when they first met. During her expedition, Aloha crossed through forty-three countries and four continents, thus realising her dream to travel and experience adventure. Of course, between the world wars, the world was experiencing rapid political and industrial change. Aloha explored World War I battlefields as she swept across France, and in Italy, Mussolini and his Fascist regime were embarking on their rise to power. Events in Germany also exposed Aloha to the frightening prospect of mobs and hostile riots which were taking place. Germany was recovering from the financial crisis after the war, and the social unrest this crisis caused gave rise to the emergence of Hitler and Fascism. Aloha travelled to Africa, passing through Egypt and into the Palestinian state at the time the Jewish peoples were settling into the region in increasing numbers. Her journey took her on to India, where she witnessed the cultural underpinnings of a population heavily influenced by their various religious strictures and practices, cultures which were often in vast contrast to the influence of their British colonials. Her journey was not only exciting, but it also exposed her to considerable danger; she nearly died of thirst in the Sudanese desert. Disguising herself as a man, she also had the chance to pray in Mecca. Her journey was remarkable from hunting elephants in Indochina to becoming a confidante of Chinese bandits. She even found time to marry Captain Wanderwell in California. The couple gained international recognition when they released a documentary after completing their trek across the globe.

Aloha was not only a traveller and adventurer but, as we can see from her documentary, also a filmmaker. Her first world tour did not sate her thirst for travel; over twenty-five years, she could visit fifty countries, thus becoming known as the World's Most Widely Traveled Girl. The significance of her global exploration is made all the greater in that she was not just a wealthy observer but interacted with various cultures and people to further both her own learning and that of the people she visited. She also joined with her husband to promote the Work Around the World Educational Club, which was a platform to spread peace at a global level through the use of education and disarmament. They worked on this ambitious project until Captain Wanderwell's death, after which Aloha continued to produce films and work as a travelling lecturer, speaking at many locations around the world.

Aloha can be remembered as a symbol of strength, hope, and courage. She traversed the world, promoting her message of love, peace, and collaboration. She used the vital tool of education to help others through the use of lectures and her travelogues. She played a significant part in the promotion of global unity and harmony.

RACHEL CARSON (1907–1964)

American Biologist Known for Her Influential Writings on Environmental Pollution and the Natural History of the Sea

It was with the publication of her book *Silent Spring* in 1962 that Rachel Carson began to really be noticed. And not always in a good way. Even though she was already a renowned writer, suddenly, her subject hit a nerve.

Rachel had developed her love of the natural environment from her mother (she grew up on a farm, the youngest of three siblings) and turned to writing to share her learning. Indeed, she was a prolific author right from her early days. Her first article was published in a children's magazine when she was only ten. As she became older, Rachel polished her skills and became a specialist in zoology. She would have pursued a doctorate in the field, but her family were experiencing financial difficulties as the US economy deflated, and she needed to earn some money to support her mother and the two nieces for whom her mother was caring. In turn, this led her to be recruited by the US Bureau of Fisheries, only the second woman ever to be employed by the institution. She remained there for fifteen years and contributed to the writings and publications of the US Fish and Wildlife Service.

She published several successful books, including one serialised in the New Yorker, and became a well-regarded author in the field. *Under the Sea-Wind* and *The Sea Around Us* were two of these publications. Indeed, her interest in the oceans was at the forefront of her mind, and she also published *The Edge of the Sea*. She won many awards, including the Guggenheim Grant, a national book award and a national science writing prize.

A series of life-changing circumstances conspired to bring about *Silent Spring*. Following the death of a niece in 1957, she adopted her great nephew and moved to Silver Spring in Maryland, there to bring up the child and also care for her now an elderly mother. It was then that she received a letter from a friend. The letter outlined how bird numbers had dropped following the spraying of insecticides. Rachel became very interested and investigated. What she found formed the basis of

Silent Spring. She discovered these pesticides were severely impacting on ecosystems. But there was more. They were also stated in the rise in several cancers, and she believed that corruption allowed this to occur. She accused the chemicals industry of spreading misinformation and public officials of failing to pay due diligence to chemical industry claims and requests.

The chemical industry was a powerful body in the late 1950s and early 1960s and set about smearing Rachel's name. Since they had no proven facts to deny her claims, they decided the only option was to discredit her. Employing political bias and misogyny as a powerful dual weapon, they stated she was a communist (an easy-to-make and common accusation against anybody seeking to hold others to account in those days) and a hysterical woman. When CBS released a documentary report on Rachel's book, they withdrew their advertising from the channel.

But people were becoming sick of the bullying, lies and profiteering of major commercial institutions and the unwillingness of elected representatives to hold them to account. Millions tuned in to watch the programme, and President Kennedy ordered an investigation. Its findings validated Rachel's research.

She received awards from both the National Audubon Society and the American Geographical Institute and was inducted into the American Academy of Arts of Letters. Sadly, though, Rachel was already very ill with breast cancer and died shortly after the publication of her book. Still, in 1980, she was awarded the Presidential Medal of Freedom.

Rachel really was a remarkable woman. Her life was driven by care for her family, and she was completely altruistic in putting these people first. She was a proper environmental campaigner, telling the truth and educating people in an easy and approachable way. She stood up to the bullying and intimidation of the chemical industry, even while she was very ill herself.

Without question, by forcing the chemical industry to adopt safer policies and practices in producing its pesticides, her findings and their publication saved tens of thousands of lives.

DIAN FOSSEY (1932–1985)

An American Conservationist Pioneer Who Studied and Protected the Lives of Mountain Gorillas

There's no doubt about it, Dian Fossey could be a tough woman. In fact, she was usually hard to be around. Shy and awkward, she broke her ankle on her first trip to Africa, stumbling over a fossil. She was not the greatest of company unless you were a mountain gorilla.

In fact, it appears Dian always preferred the company of animals over that of humans. Her first interest was horses, and she wanted to become a vet. But if she could be a challenging company, there is no question regarding her dedication. Or her intelligence. Somehow, she ended up in occupational therapy and became director of the Kosair Crippled Children's Hospital based in Kentucky.

But this was not her calling. In fact, she did not know what she wanted in life. Until she saved up and booked a flight to Africa, there she met the archaeologist Mary Leakey and her husband, Louis. She had then travelled to a nearby gorilla reserve. She knew nothing of these astonishing beasts but fell in love with them at once. She would end up dedicating her life to them literally, as it turned out. Three years after that initial visit, Louis was in Louisville and sought out Dian. He could see that, despite her important position at her clinic, something was missing from her life. He asked to speak to her and offered her the chance to become his 'Gorilla Girl'. She accepted at once. It was 1966, and Dian was about to spend nineteen years studying, protecting, and befriending mountain gorillas.

The primates lived in a protected reserve high in the Virunga Mountains, on the border with Rwanda, Uganda and what is now the Democratic Republic of the Congo. Protected? In theory only. The gorillas were victims of poachers, who often worked with those guards paid to preserve the magnificent beasts. Numbers were falling. Fast.

Living in sheet metal cabins high in the steaming mountains, Dian grew to love the gorillas. She found them tolerant, brilliant parents, intelligent and loving. Although students and scientists visited from time to time, and she had to endure unwanted tourists who at least brought money along with them, in her opinion, stupidity, it was the gorillas she adored and felt most comfortable among. It was they with whom she spent the most time. She endured the company of humans but enjoyed her contact with the gorillas. Still, the poachers held sway. Despite her best efforts, the gorilla population halved in the twenty years from 1960, when they had previously been studied. But Dian's efforts turned the corner. In 1983, she published *Gorillas in the Mist*, a magical book about her life with the animals.

Two years later, she was dead. Most probably murdered by the poachers she opposed.

Dian's life shows that a woman does not have to be socially adept at making a difference. She does not have to say the right things or meet the right people. With dedication, commitment and a clear aim in life, she can leave her mark.

But what about the most important aspect of Dian's life? Those mountain gorillas? When she carried out a formal count in 1981, the numbers were down to just 240. It was widely assumed that by the end of the millennium, the mountain gorilla would have joined so many other species wiped out by the actions of man.

They were not made extinct. Today, nearly seven hundred live in those mountains and more than a thousand across Africa. Dian's commitment paid off. She saved the mountain gorilla.

MAVYNEE BETSCH (1935–2005)

Beach Lady
American Environmentalist who Made It Her Full-Time Mission to Preserve and Protect American Beach

American Beach, MaVynee Betsch's great-grandfather's investment, was threatened by development and, therefore, destruction. Her unstinting efforts and dedication to save the Florida beach and its inhabitants earned her the sobriquet 'Beach Lady'.

MaVynee was an opera singer by trade and an environmental activist by choice. She was totally committed to her cause of acting as an eco-friendly enthusiast. Indeed, she became a lifelong member of several environmental organisations, many of which were involved in the conservation of the animal species in her beach environment.

Not only was she committed to the environment, but MaVynee was also a great philanthropist. She gave away her life savings to be shared among over sixty environmental organisations. She had been raised by an eminent black family in the south of the US and took advantage of her family background to work on the cause of conserving the environment and making it more eco-friendly. She was also a prominent advocate for the value of what nature can provide and was involved in promoting this view. For example, her hair and nails were left to grow naturally for over twenty years, thus illustrating that nature, if preserved, can be a key factor in human growth. As an illustration of her perspective, she saw no need for humans to supplement their bodies with protein from meat.

Lady Beach worked for causes which benefited the entire community. This included her development of extensive plans to protect American Beach. Despite the prevalence of Jim Crow laws at the time and white prejudice against the black community, which made it hard to further her aims, MaVynee made tremendous leaps forward in the environmental field. Later, her work was acclaimed by the international community and all racial groups.

MaVynee was diagnosed with cancer, which led to the removal of her stomach but did not let this serious illness stop her from working for the protection of the environment. Her resolve to conserve American Beach acts as a symbol to provide massive inspiration to people to pursue their dreams and goals even when facing opposition from other sections of society.

WANGARI MAATHAI (1940–2011)

Environmentalist, Political Activist and the First Black African Woman to Win a Nobel Prize

Being taken seriously as a woman can be difficult. Certainly, that was the case for Wangari Maathai in her traditional Kenyan community. She held strong political views and was a committed environmental activist, but her work could often be viewed derisively because of traditional gender roles in her society, where women were frequently relegated to a subservient position. Wangari had no intention of tolerating that. Which, unsurprisingly, made her unpopular among the male elite.

However, these societal barriers did not stop Maathai from pursuing her dreams. She became the first woman in East and Central Africa to receive a doctorate in biological sciences. She was also interested in veterinary anatomy and indeed taught the subject at the University of Nairobi. She also became the first woman to earn the position of an associate professor and chair of the Department of Veterinary Anatomy, which she achieved in the 1970s.

Wangari gained inspiration from the civil rights movement. During her time as a member of the National Council of Women of Kenya, she promoted the idea of planting trees at a large enough rate to improve air quality. She worked with the help of a group of women on the project, which culminated in the Green Belt Movement. This scheme for the conservation of the ecosystem earned global acclaim and resulted in the planting of twenty million trees.

Wangari's fame also grew because of her resolute opposition to land-grabbing developers. She promoted the protection of water reservoirs and green spaces in Kenya and led a movement to construct a public recreational park. Apart from her environmental activism, Wangari was particularly politically astute, engaging in the replacement of one-party rule in Kenya with a multi-party democratic system. Leading the Release Political Prisoners (RPP) group, along with other women, she protested passionately for releasing people detained and confined illegally and denied any right to a fair trial. Their protest continued for eleven months, and the women went to the extent of stripping naked when security officers tried to sabotage their protest.

Thus, Wangari contributed much to the welfare of the environment and the people in her homeland of Kenya. Her work, though, held a wider impact. The environmental advances she made brought global benefit to life on Earth.

BIBLIOGRAPHY

"Alice Coachman." *United States Olympic & Paralympic Museum*, https://usopm.org/alice-coachman/.

"Amelia Earhart, Queen of the Air." *Nasa.Gov*, https://www.nasa.gov/sites/default/files/atoms/files/amelia-earhart-ms-view.pdf.

"Amelia Earhart." *Biography*, 2018, https://www.biography.com/explorer/amelia-earhart.

Atwood, Kathryn J. *Women Heroes of World War II: 26 Stories of Espionage, Sabotage, Resistance, And Rescue*. Chicago Review Press, 2019.

B. Clark, Elizabeth. "Self-Ownership and the Political Theory of Elizabeth Cady Stanton." *Connecticut Law Review*, vol 21, no. 905, 1989, https://core.ac.uk/download/pdf/229123726.pdf. Accessed 25 Feb 2021.

Baker, Aloha Wanderwell, and Idris Galcia Hall. *Aloha Wanderwell "Call to Adventure": True Tales of the Wanderwell Expedition, First Woman to Circle the World in an Automobile*. Nile Baker Estate & Boyd Production Group, 2013.

Basu, Shrabani. *Spy Princess the Life of Noor Inayat Khan*. The History Press, 2011.

"Bessie Coleman." Pbs.Org, https://www.pbs.org/wgbh/americanexperience/features/flygirls-bessie-coleman/.

Biedzynski, James. "Empress Dowager Cixi: The Concubine Who Launched Modern China." *Journal of Third World Studies*, vol 32, no. 1, 2015.

Bilvao, Pulgarin and Paola, Lissette. "Irena Sendler. A Nurse Example of Love of Freedom." *Investigación Y Educación En Enfermería*, vol 30, no. 2, 2012, https://www.researchgate.net/publication/260772892_Irena_Sendler_A_nurse_example_of_love_of_freedom. Accessed 26 Feb 2021.

Bowen, Shannon A. "Finding Strategic Communication & Diverse Leadership in the Ancient World: The Case of Queen Cleopatra VII, the Last Pharaoh of Egypt." *Cogent Arts & Humanities*, vol 3, no. 1, 2016, p. 1154704. *Informa UK Limited*, doi:10.1080/23311983.2016.1154704. Accessed 25 Feb 2021.

Buckle, Georgina et al. "Powerful Northern Women: Lilian Bader - Northern Power Women." Northern Power Women, https://www.northernpowerwomen.com/powerful-northern-women-lilian-bader/.

Callender, Vivianne. "Hatshepsut." *The Encyclopaedia of Ancient History*, 2012. *Blackwell Publishing Ltd*, doi:10.1002/9781444338386.wbeah15187. Accessed 25 Feb 2021.

Cannon, Geoffrey. "Wangari Maathai. Speaking and Acting for Africa." *World Public Health Nutrition Association*, 2011, Accessed 26 Feb 2021.

Cara, Elizabeth. "An Example of Occupational Coherence: The Story of Dian Fossey, Occupational Therapist and Primatologist." *British Journal of Occupational Therapy*, vol 70, no. 4, 2007, pp. 147–153. SAGE Publications, doi:10.1177/030802260707000403. Accessed 26 Feb 2021.

Carpentier, Florence. "Alice Milliat: A Feminist Pioneer for Women's Sport." *Global Sports Leaders*, 2018, pp. 61-81. Springer International Publishing, doi:10.1007/978-3-319-76753-6_3. Accessed 30 Jan 2021.

Carter-Ényì, Quintina, and Aaron Carter-Ényì. "Decolonizing the Mind Through Song: From Makeba to the Afropolitan Present." *Performance Research*, vol 24, no. 1, 2019, pp. 58-65. *Informa UK Limited*, doi:10.1080/13528165.2019.1593737. Accessed 7 Mar 2021.

Cascone, Sarah. "Who Is Fanny Eaton? The Jamaican Model Who Inspired the Pre-Raphaelites Is the Latest Art Figure to Get a Google Doodle." Artnet News, 2020, https://news.artnet.com/art-world/meet-jamaican-model-pre-raphaelites-fanny-eaton–1924659.

Celebrating African American Inventors & Innovators. Orange County Regional History Center, http://www.thehistorycenter.org/wp-content/uploads/2017/01/AA_Inventors_booklet_lo.pdf. Accessed 30 Jan 2021.

Cha, John. *Willow Tree Shade: The Susan Ahn Cuddy Story*. Korean American Heritage Foundation, 2005.

Charman-Anderson, Suw. "Ada Lovelace: A Simple Solution to a Lengthy Controversy." *Patterns*, vol 1, no. 7, 2020, p. 100118. Elsevier BV, doi:10.1016/j.patter.2020.100118. Accessed 30 Jan 2021.

Chayer, Mary Ella. "Mary Eliza Mahoney." *American Journal of Nursing*, vol 54, no. 4, 1954, Accessed 3 Mar 2021.

Coffee, Alan M. S. J. "Mary Wollstonecraft, Freedom and the Enduring Power of Social Domination." *European Journal of Political Theory*, vol 12, no. 2, 2012, pp. 116–135. SAGE Publications, doi:10.1177/1474885111430617. Accessed 25 Feb 2021.

Cohen, Daniel. "Boudicca's Rebellion Against the Roman Empire in 60 AD." Union College Digital Works, 2016, https://digitalworks.union.edu/cgi/viewcontent.cgi?article=1134&context=theses. Accessed 25 Feb 2021.

Cornelsen, Kathleen. "Women Airforce Service Pilots of World War II: Exploring Military Aviation, Encountering Discrimination, and Exchanging Traditional Roles in Service to America." *Journal of Women's History*, vol 17, no. 4, 2005, pp. 111–119. *Project Muse*, doi:10.1353/jowh.2005.0046. Accessed 26 Feb 2021.

Crewe, Sandra Edmonds. "Harriet Tubman: Peacemaker and Stateswoman." *Affilia*, vol 21, no. 2, 2006, pp. 228–233. SAGE Publications, doi:10.1177/0886109905285773. Accessed 25 Feb 2021.

Curtis, Lara R. "Noor Inayat Khan: Conceptualizing Resistance During World War II." *Writing Resistance and the Question of Gender*, 2019, pp. 59-94. Springer International Publishing, doi:10.1007/978-3-030-31242-8_3. Accessed 26 Feb 2021.

Czarnecki, Kristin, and Carrie Rohman. *Virginia Woolf and the Natural World*. Liverpool University Press, 2011.

Darraj, Susan Muaddi. *Mary Eliza Mahoney and the Legacy of African-American Nurses (Women in Medicine)*. Chelsea House Publications, 2004.

Davies, Carole Boyce. *Left Of Karl Marx – The Political Life of Black Communist Claudia Jones*. Duke University Press, 2008.

Deakin, Michael. "Hypatia and Her Mathematics." *The American Mathematical Monthly*, vol 101, no. 3, 1994, Accessed 30 Jan 2021.

DePrest, Jessica. "Aloha Wanderwell Baker." *Women Film Pioneers Project*, 2018. *Columbia Academic Commons*, Accessed 26 Feb 2021.

Dever, Maryanne. "Greta Garbo's Foot, or Sex, Socks, and Letters." *Australian Feminist Studies*, vol 25, no. 64, 2010, pp. 163–173. Informa UK Limited, doi:10.1080/08164641003762461. Accessed 25 Feb 2021.

Doran, Susan, and Norman Jones. "The Elizabethan World." *The Queen*, 2010, Accessed 25 Feb 2021.

"Dorothy Hodgkin –1964 Nobel Laureate for Work on Vitamin B." *Mayo Foundation for Medical Education and Research*, vol 77, no.

403, 2002, https://www.mayoclinicproceedings.org/article/S0025-6196(11)62206-4/pdf. Accessed 30 Jan 2021.

DuBois, Ellen Carol, and Elizabeth Cady Stanton. *Elizabeth Cady Stanton, Feminist as Thinker*. New York University Press, 2007.

Duman, Faith. "The Roots of Modern Feminism: Mary Wollstonecraft and the French Revolution." *International Journal of Humanities and Social Science*, vol 2, no. 9, 2012, pp. 38-42., https://www.researchgate.net/publication/312939904_The_Roots_of_Modern_Feminism_Mary_Wollstonecraft_and_the_French_Revolution.

E. Delaney, Angelica. "Reading Cleopatra VII: The Crafting of a Political Persona." *The Kennesaw Journal of Undergraduate Research*, vol 3, no. 1, 2014, https://www.academia.edu/6708239/Reading_Cleopatra_VII_The_Crafting_of_a_Political_Persona. Accessed 25 Feb 2021.

E. Slotnik, Daniel. "Overlooked No More: Bessie Coleman, Pioneering African-American Aviatrix." *NY Times*, 2019, https://www.nytimes.com/2019/12/11/obituaries/bessie-coleman-overlooked.html. Accessed 30 Jan 2021.

Eylott, Marie-Claire. "Mary Anning: The Unsung Hero of Fossil Discovery." *Nhm. Ac. Uk*, https://www.nhm.ac.uk/discover/mary-anning-unsung-hero.html.

Ferry, Georgina, and Eugenie V. Mielczarek. "Dorothy Hodgkin: A Life." *Physics Today*, vol 53, no. 4, 2000, pp. 68-69. AIP Publishing, doi:10.1063/1.883052. Accessed 30 Jan 2021.

Figes, Lydia. "Fanny Eaton: Jamaican Pre-Raphaelite Muse | Art UK." Artuk.Org, 2019, https://artuk.org/discover/stories/fanny-eaton-jamaican-pre-raphaelite-muse.

Flori, Jean. *Eleanor of Aquitaine: Queen and Rebel.* Edinburgh University Press, 2007.

Forristal, Linda Joyce. "On the Trail of Joan of Arc." *Journal of Tourism, Culture and Territorial Development*, 2013, https://www.researchgate.net/publication/307707497_On_the_Trail_of_Joan_of_Arc. Accessed 26 Feb 2021.

Frank, Katherine. "The Lives of Indira Gandhi." *Women's Lives into Print*, 1999, pp. 152–169. Palgrave Macmillan UK, doi:10.1057/9780230374577_11. Accessed 25 Feb 2021.

Gabbay, Alyssa. "In Reality a Man: Sultan Iltutmish, His Daughter, Raziya, and Gender Ambiguity in Thirteenth-Century Northern India." *Journal of Persianate Studies*, vol 4, no. 1, 2011, pp. 45-63. Brill, doi:10.1163/187471611x568285.

Gates, Eugene. "Clara Schumann: A Composer's Wife as Composer." *The Kapralova Society Journal*, vol 7, no. 2, 2009, https://www.researchgate.net/publication/329655858_Clara_Schumann_A_Composer's_Wife_as_Composer. Accessed 26 Feb 2021.

Gems, Gerald R. *Before Jackie Robinson: The Transcendent Role of Black Sporting Pioneers*. University Of Nebraska Press, 2017.

"Gertrude Ederle Becomes First Woman to Swim English Channel." History, 2009, https://www.history.com/this-day-in-history/gertrude-ederle-becomes-first-woman-to-swim-english-channel.

Gill, Jo. "Gwendolyn Brooks and the Legacies of Architectural Modernity." *Humanities*, vol 8, no. 4, 2019, p. 167. *MDPI AG*, doi:10.3390/h8040167. Accessed 25 Feb 2021.

Grades, Erlangung des akademischen. "Traveling Women Professionals: A Transnational Perspective on Mobility and Professionalism of Four Women at the End of the Nineteenth and the Beginning of the Twentieth Century." Der Universität Rostock, 2018.

Gregory, Tsoucalas et al. "Metrodora, an Innovative Gynaecologist, Midwife, and Surgeon." *Surgical Innovation*, vol 20, no. 6, 2013, pp. 648-649. SAGE Publications, doi:10.1177/1553350613485304. Accessed 30 Jan 2021.

Gregory, Tsoucalas, and Sgantzos Markos. "Aspasia and Cleopatra Metrodora, Two Majestic Female Physician Surgeons in the Early Byzantine Era." *Journal of Universal Surgery*, 2016, https://www.jusurgery.com/universalsurgery/aspasia-and-cleopatra-metrodora-twomajestic-female-physician--surgeons-in-theearly-byzantine-era.php?aid=11083. Accessed 30 Jan 2021.

H. Adams, Katherine, and Michael L. Keene. *Alice Paul and the American Suffrage Campaign*. University of Illinois Press, 2008.

H. Allison, Fred. "Jacqueline Cochran: Biography of a Pioneer Aviator." *AirPower History*, vol 65, no. 2, 2018, Accessed 26 Feb 2021.

H. Bradford, Sarah. *Harriet, the Moses of Her People.* 1886.

Haigh, Christopher. *The Reign of Elizabeth I.* Macmillan, 1984.

Hausfater, Glenn, and Kenneth A. R. Kennedy. "Dian Fossey, (1932–1985)." *American Anthropologist*, vol 88, no. 4, 1986, pp. 953-956. Wiley, doi:10.1525/aa.1986.88.4.02a00140. Accessed 26 Feb 2021.

Hawranick, Sylvia et al. "Alice Paul." *Affilia*, vol 23, no. 2, 2008, pp. 190–196. SAGE Publications, doi:10.1177/0886109908314332. Accessed 25 Feb 2021.

Hill, Rebecca. "Marie Van Brittan Brown (1922–1999)." Blackpast.Org, 2016, https://www.blackpast.org/african-american-history/brown-marie-van-brittan–1922–1999/.

Hilliard, Kristina, and Kate Wurtzel. "Power and Gender in Ancient Egypt: The Case of Hatshepsut." *Art Education*, vol 62, no. 3, 2009, pp. 25-31. Informa UK Limited, doi:10.1080/00043125.2009.11519017. Accessed 25 Feb 2021.

Hollings, Christopher et al. "The Early Mathematical Education of Ada Lovelace." *Journal of the British Society for the History of Mathematics*, 2017, https://www.claymath.org/sites/default/files/the_early_mathematical_education_of_ada_lovelace.pdf. Accessed 30 Jan 2021.

Hyla Whittaker, Cynthia. "Catherine the Great and the Art of Collecting: Acquiring the Paintings That Founded the Hermitage." *Word and Image in Russian History*, 2019, pp. 147–171. Academic Studies Press, doi:10.1515/9781618117090-014. Accessed 25 Feb 2021.

Ismael, Zaid Ibrahim, and Afaf Darraji. "Harriet Beecher Stowe: A Woman Who Changed History." *Women and Society*, 2019, https://www.researchgate.net/publication/331153669_Harriet_Beecher_Stowe_A_Woman_Who_Changed_History. Accessed 26 Feb 2021.

Ivleva, Victoria. "Catherine II as Female Ruler: The Power of Enlightened Womanhood." *E-Journal of Eighteenth-Century Russian Studies*, vol 3, 2015, pp. 20-46., https://www.academia.edu/15424131/Catherine_II_as_Female_Ruler_The_Power_of_Enlightened_Womanhood. Accessed 25 Feb 2021.

J Basil, Christine, and Rachel K Alexander. "Mark Twain's Joan of Arc: An American Woman?" *A Journal of Political Philosophy*, vol 44, no. 2, 2018, https://www.academia.edu/35987944/Mark_Twains_Joan_of_Arc_An_American_Woman. Accessed 26 Feb 2021.

J. Meyr, Jessica. "Grace Hopper and the Marvelous Machine: Lessons for Modern Technical Communicators from the Mark I ASCC Manual." University of Central Florida, 2017.

J. Petty, Miria. *Stealing the Show: African American Performers and Audiences in 1930s Hollywood*. University of California Press, 2016.

Jamison, Angelene. "Analysis of Selected Poetry of Phillis Wheatley." *The Journal of Negro Education*, vol 43, no. 3, 1974, p. 408. JSTOR, doi:10.2307/2966532. Accessed 7 Mar 2021.

Jochens, Jenny. "Gudrid Thorbjarnardottir." *Clio*, no. 28, 2008, pp. 38-58. Open edition, doi:10.4000/clio.7703. Accessed 26 Feb 2021.

Johnson, Connie. "Reclaiming Claudia Jones: When a Black Feminist Marxist Defies McCarthyism." *Michigan Feminist Studies*, https://quod.lib.umich.edu/cgi/p/pod/dod-idx/reclaiming-claudia-jones-when-a-black-feminist-marxist.pdf?c=mfs-front;idno=ark5583.0022.102;format=pdf. Accessed 7 Mar 2021.

Johnson-Miller, Beverly C. "Mary McLeod Bethune: Black Educational Ministry Leader of the Early Twentieth Century." *Christian Education Journal: Research on Educational Ministry*, vol 3, no. 2, 2006, pp. 330-342. SAGE Publications, doi:10.1177/073989130600300208. Accessed 25 Feb 2021.

Jones, Clara. *Virginia Woolf: Ambivalent Activist*. Edinburgh University Press, 2016.

Jukić, Tatjana. "The October Garbo: Classical Hollywood and the Revolution." *Studia Litterarum*, vol 2, no. 2, 2017, pp. 56-63. *A. M. Gorky Institute of World Literature of the Russian Academy of Sciences*, doi:10.22455/2500-4247–2017–2–2-56-63.

Kafarowski, Joanna. "From Boots On 'Till Boots Off: Collecting Greenland with Explorer Louise Arner Boyd." *The Polar Adventures of a Rich American Dame: A Life of Louise Arner Boyd*, 2019, Accessed 26 Feb 2021.

Kaim, Chanchal. *Indira Gandhi – Iron Lady of India*. Lap Lambert Academic Publ, 2011.

Kanogo, Tabitha M. *Wangari Maathai*. Ohio University Press, 2020.

Kaosar Ahmed, Mohammad. "Mother Teresa's Godlessness for the Last Four Decades of Her Life: Hypocrisy or Spiritual Heroism?" *Darul Ihsan University Studies*, vol 2, 2007, Accessed 30 Jan 2021.

Karimi, Hosein, and Negin Masoudi Alavi. "Florence Nightingale: The Mother of Nursing." *Nursing and Midwifery Studies*, vol 4, no. 2, 2015. Medknow, doi:10.17795/nmsjournal29475. Accessed 30 Jan 2021.

Keatley, Rachel. "Happy Birthday, Marie Van Brittan Brown." *COMSOL Multiphysics*, 2020, https://www.comsol.com/blogs/happy-birthday-marie-van-brittan-brown/.

Kerstetter, N. "The Silent Spring of Rachel Carson." *OAH Magazine of History*, vol 10, no. 3, 1996, pp. 25–27. *Oxford University Press (OUP)*, doi:10.1093/maghis/10.3.25. Accessed 26 Feb 2021.

Kroll, Gary. "The 'Silent Springs' of Rachel Carson: Mass Media and the Origins of Modern Environmentalism." *Public Understanding of Science*, vol 10, no. 4, 2001, pp. 403-420. SAGE Publications, doi:10.1088/0963-6625/10/4/304. Accessed 26 Feb 2021.

L. Mitchell, Carmen. "The Contributions of Grace Murray Hopper to Computer Science and Computer Education." University of North Texas, 1994.

L. Quigley, Samantha. "Women of War." Bt.Royle.com, 2015, http://bt.royle.com/article/WOMEN+OF+WAR/2247046/269684/article.html.

"Lady Grace Drummond-Hay | Airships.Net." Airships.Net, https://www.airships.net/airship-people/lady-grace-drummond-hay/.

Law, Dr. Kate. "Lilian Bader: One of the First Black British Women in the Royal Air Force by Lucia Wallbank." Women's History Network, 2020, https://womenshistorynetwork.org/lilian-bader-one-of-the-first-black-british-women-in-the-royal-air-force-by-lucia-wallbank/.

Lee Alexander, Kerri. "Bessie Coleman." National Women's History Museum, 2018, https://www.womenshistory.org/education-resources/biographies/bessie-coleman.

Leffall, Dolores C., and Janet L. Sims. "Mary McLeod Bethune – The Educator; Also Including a Selected Annotated Bibliography." *The Journal of Negro Education*, vol 45, no. 3, 1976, p. 342. *JSTOR*, doi:10.2307/2966912. Accessed 25 Feb 2021.

Lepekhova, Elena. "Empresses and Buddhism in Japan in VI–VIII cc." *Journal of Cultural and Religious Studies*, vol 4, no. 1, 2016. David Publishing Company, doi:10.17265/2328–2177/2016.01.005. Accessed 25 Feb 2021.

Letort, D., 2012. *The Rosa Parks Story: The Making of a Civil Rights Icon*. Black Camera, [online] 3(2). Available at: <https://www.jstor.org/stable/pdf/10.2979/blackcamera.3.2.31.pdf> [Accessed 25 February 2021].

Levin, Carole. *Remembering Queens and Kings of Early Modern England and France*. Palgrave Macmillan, Cham, 2019.

Lewis, Desiree. "Claudia Jones: Beyond Containment Autobiographical Reflections, Essays and Poems, Edited by Carole Boyce Davies." *Agenda*, vol 25, no. 4, 2011, pp. 118–120. *Informa UK Limited*, doi:10.1080/10130950.2011.633398. Accessed 7 Mar 2021.

"Lily Parr, the Pioneering Star." www.fifa.com, 2020, https://www.fifa.com/news/lily-parr-the-pioneering-star–2593969.

"Lily Parr." Nationalfootballmuseum.com, https://www.nationalfootballmuseum.com/halloffame/lily-parr/.

"Lily Parr." Spartacus Educational, https://spartacus-educational.com/FparrL.htm.

Looser, Devoney. "Jane Austen Camp." *ABO: Interactive Journal for Women in the Arts*, vol 9, no. 1, 2019. The University of South Florida Libraries, doi:10.5038/2157-7129.9.1.1172. Accessed 25 Feb 2021.

Luscombe, A., 2018. Eleanor Roosevelt: A Crusading Spirit to Move Human Rights Forward. *Netherlands Quarterly of Human Rights*, [online] 36(4), pp.241–246. Available at:

<https://journals.sagepub.com/doi/pdf/10.1177/0924051918801610>
[Accessed 25 February 2021].

Lynn Patino, Frankie. "Well-Behaved Women Rarely Make History: An Examination of the Life of Jacqueline Cochran." California State University, 2020.

M. Bulst, Christoph. "The Revolt of Queen Boudicca in AD 60." *Historia: Zeitschrift Für Alte Geschichte*, vol 10, no. 4, 1961, https://www.jstor.org/stable/4434717?seq=1. Accessed 25 Feb 2021.

M. Parker, Alison. "The Picture of Health: The Public Life and Private Ailments of Mary Church Terrell." *Journal of Historical Biography*, vol 13, 2013, https://digitalcommons.brockport.edu/cgi/viewcontent.cgi?article=1007&context=hst_facpub. Accessed 25 Feb 2021.

MacAloon, John J. *This Great Symbol: Pierre De Coubertin and the Origins of the Olympic Games*. The University of Chicago Press, 1981.

Malaspina, Ann, and Eric Velasquez. *Touch The Sky: Alice Coachman Olympic High Jumper*. Av2 By Weigl, 2014.

Marie Sanz, Crickette, and David Morgan. "Dian Fossey." *Encyclopedia of Animal Cognition and Behavior*, 2017, Accessed 26 Feb 2021.

Mark, Joshua. "Hypatia of Alexandria." *Ancient History Encyclopedia*, 2009, https://www.ancient.eu/Hypatia_of_Alexandria/.

"Mary Eliza Mahoney, First Negro Nurse." Vol 46, no. 4, 1954, Accessed 3 Mar 2021.

Mateos Padorno, Covadonga et al. "An Approach to the Historical Development of Female Athletics in the Olympic Games." *Journal of Human Sport and Exercise*, vol 5, no. 2, 2010, pp. 117–126. *Journal of Human Sport and Exercise*, doi:10.4100/jhse.2010.52.02.

"MaVynee 'Beach Lady' Betsch's Biography." The Historymakers, 2004, https://www.thehistorymakers.org/biography/mavynee-beach-lady-betsch-39.

Mazzeo, Tilar J. *Irena's Children*. Simon & Schuster, 2016.

McCluskey, Audrey Thomas. "Mary McLeod Bethune and the Education of Black Girls." *Sex Roles*, vol 21, no. 1–2, 1989, pp. 113–126. Springer Science and Business Media LLC, doi:10.1007/bf00289731. Accessed 25 Feb 2021.

Medeiros, Ana Beatriz de Almeida et al. "The Florence Nightingale's Environmental Theory: A Critical Analysis." *Escola Anna Nery*, vol 19, no. 3, 2015. Fapunifesp (Scielo), doi:10.5935/1414-8145.20150069.

Melhem, D. H. *Gwendolyn Brooks: Poetry and the Heroic Voice*. The University Press of Kentucky, 2015.

Merish, Lori. "Sentimental Consumption: Harriet Beecher Stowe and the Aesthetics of Middle-Class Ownership." *American Literary*

History, vol 8, no. 1, 1996, pp. 1-33. Oxford University Press (OUP), doi:10.1093/alh/8.1.1.

"Metrodora, Physician (Practiced Around 200-400 CE)." Targethealth.com, 2019, https://www.targethealth.com/post/metrodora-physician-practiced-around–200-400-ce.

Michals, Debra. "Mildred 'Babe' Didrikson Zaharias." National Women's History Museum, 2015, https://www.womenshistory.org/education-resources/biographies/mildred-zaharias.

"Mother Teresa." Biography, 2017, https://www.biography.com/religious-figure/mother-teresa.

Mould, R. F. "Marie and Pierre Curie and Radium: History, Mystery, and Discovery." *Medical Physics*, vol 26, no. 9, 1999, pp. 1766–1772. Wiley, doi:10.1118/1.598680.

O'Brien, C. C. "The White Women All Go for Sex: Frances Harper on Suffrage, Citizenship, and the Reconstruction South." *African American Review*, vol 43, no. 4, 2009, pp. 605-620. Project Muse, doi:10.1353/afa.2009.0056.

O'Farrell, B., 2010. *She Was One of Us: Eleanor Roosevelt and the American Worker*. Ithaca: Cornell University Press.

Owen, David. "The Suffragettes of Sport – Alice Milliat and the Rebel Pioneers of Twentieth-Century Women's Athletics."

Insidethegames.biz, 2016, https://www.insidethegames.biz/articles/1035085/the-suffragettes-of-sport-alice-milliat-and-the-rebel-pioneers-of–twentieth-century-womens-athletics.

Parčina, Ivana et al. "Women's World Games." *Physical Education and Sport Through the Centuries*, vol 1, no. 2, 2014, pp. 49-60., http://www.fiep-serbia.net/docs/vol–1-i–2/en/paper-5.pdf. Accessed 30 Jan 2021.

Parks, V., 2016. "Rosa Parks Redux: Racial Mobility Projects on the Journey to Work." *Annals of the American Association of Geographers*, [online] pp.1-8. <https://www.researchgate.net/publication/292328276_Rosa_Parks_Redux_Racial_Mobility_Projects_on_the_Journey_to_Work. Accessed 25 February 2021.

Petry, Ann et al. *Harriet Tubman: Conductor on the Underground Railroad*. HarperCollins Publishers, 2018.

"Phillis Wheatley | Poetry Foundation." Poetry Foundation, https://www.poetryfoundation.org/poets/phillis-wheatley.

Piirto, Jane. *Ella Fitzgerald*. Academic Press, 2011.

Potter, Sean. "Retrospect: May 20, 1932: Amelia Earhart's Solo Transatlantic Flight." *Weatherwise*, vol 63, no. 3, 2010, pp. 13–14. Informa UK Limited, doi:10.1080/00431671003732598. Accessed 30 Jan 2021.

Proskurina, Vera. *Creating the Empress: Politics and Poetry in the Age of Catherine II.* Academic Studies Press, 2011.

R. Norwood, Arlisha. "Wilma Rudolph." *National Women's History Museum*, 2017, https://www.womenshistory.org/education-resources/biographies/wilma-rudolph.

Rangarajan, Mahesh. "Striving for a Balance: Nature, Power, Science and India's Indira Gandhi, 1917–1984." *Conservation and Society*, vol 7, no. 4, 2009, p. 299. Medknow, doi:10.4103/0972-4923.65175. Accessed 25 Feb 2021.

Ravell-Pinto, T. and Ravell, R., 2008. "Obituary: African Icon: Miriam 'Mama Africa' Makeba, Dies at Age 76." *Journal of the African Literature Association*, [online] 2(2), pp.274–281. Available at: <https://www.tandfonline.com/doi/abs/10.1080/21674736.2008.1169 0092?journalCode=rala20> [Accessed 7 March 2021].

"Razia Sultan of India: Queen of the World Bilqis-I Jihan." 2020, pp. 106–138. Cambridge University Press, doi:10.1017/9781316389300.005. Accessed 25 Feb 2021.

"Razia Sultan: The First and Last Woman Ruler of Delhi Sultanate | #Indianwomeninhistory." Feminism in India, https://feminisminindia.com/2017/03/17/razia-sultan-essay/.

Rédei, Anna Cabak. "Rhetoric in Film: A Cultural Semiotical Study of Greta Garbo Inninotchka." *Film International*, vol 4, no. 5, 2006, pp. 52-61. Intellect, doi:10.1386/fiin.4.5.52. Accessed 25 Feb 2021.

Reich, Nancy B. *Clara Schumann: The Artist and the Woman*. Cornell University Press, 2001.

Rickman, Sarah Byrn. *Nancy Love and the Wasp Ferry Pilots of World War II*. Univ of North Texas Press, 2014.

Ribeiro, Orquídea Moreira et al. "Nzinga Mbandi: From Story to Myth." *Journal of Science and Technology of the Arts*, vol 11, no. 1, 2019, pp. 51-60. *Universidade Catolica Portuguesa*, doi:10.7559/citarj.v11i1.594. Accessed 7 Mar 2021.

Ridley, Glynis. *The Discovery of Jeanne Baret: A Story of Science, the High Seas, and the First Woman to Circumnavigate the Globe*. Broadway Paperbacks, 2011.

Rule, Amy. "Ansel Adams and Louise Arner Boyd: A Camera Tells a Story." *History Of Photography*, vol 22, no. 2, 1998, pp. 155–160. Informa UK Limited, doi:10.1080/03087298.1998.10443871. Accessed 26 Feb 2021.

Ryall, Anka. *The Polar Adventures of a Rich American Dame: A Life of Louise Arner Boyd, By Joanna Kafarowski Toronto:© Dundurn Press, 2017, 367 Pp.,©15.99 GBP (Paperback). 5 ISBN 978–1-4597-3970-3." Polar Research*, vol 37, no. 1, 2018, p. 1492761. Norwegian Polar Institute, doi:10.1080/17518369.2018.1492761. Accessed 26 Feb 2021.

Rymer, Russ. "Beach Lady." Smithsonian Magazine, 2003, https://www.smithsonianmag.com/history/beach-lady-84237022/.

Sallah, Tijan. "Phillis Wheatley: A Brief Survey of the Life and Works of a Gambian Slave/Poet in New England America." *Wasafiri*, vol 7, no. 15, 1992, pp. 27-31. Informa UK Limited, doi:10.1080/02690059208574264. Accessed 7 Mar 2021.

Schiebinger, Londa. "Jeanne Baret: The First Woman to Circumnavigate the Globe." *Endeavour*, vol 27, no. 1, 2003, pp. 22–25. Elsevier BV, doi:10.1016/s0160-9327(03)00018-8. Accessed 26 Feb 2021.

Schwartz, Larry. "Didrikson Was a Woman Ahead of Her Time." Espn.com, https://www.espn.com/sportscentury/features/00014147.html.

Shawn Hogan, Lisa. "Sexual Exploitation in the Rhetoric of Elizabeth Cady Stanton." *CONLAWNOW*, vol 7, no. 40, 2015, https://core.ac.uk/download/pdf/232678621.pdf. Accessed 25 Feb 2021.

Shetty, Ashap. "Florence Nightingale: The Queen of Nurses." *Archives of Medicine and Health Sciences*, vol 4, no. 1, 2016, p. 144. Medknow, doi:10.4103/2321-4848.183362. Accessed 30 Jan 2021.

Siber, Kate. "The First Woman to Brave the English Channel." *Outside Online*, 2017, https://www.outsideonline.com/2265846/first-woman-brave-english-channel.

Stefanello, Vinicio. "Junko Tabei, First Woman to Summit Everest, Celebrated by Google." Planetmountain.com, 2019, https://www.planetmountain.com/en/news/alpinism/junko-tabei-first-woman-to-summit-everest-celebrated-by-google.html.

Stein, Dorothy. *Ada: A Life and a Legacy*. The MIT Press, 1987.

Sunshine, Glenn. "Christians Who Changed Their World: Gudrid Thorbjarnardóttir, 'The Far Traveler' (C.980–C.1019) – Breakpoint." Breakpoint, 2020, https://breakpoint.org/christians-who-changed-their-world-gudrid-thorbjarnardottir-the-far-traveler-c-980-c–1019/.

"Susan Ahn Cuddy, Lieutenant, US Navy – Foundation for Women Warriors." Foundation For Women Warriors, https://foundationfor-womenwarriors.org/susan-ahn-cuddy-lieutenant-u-s-navy/.

Synge, M. B. *The Reign of Queen Victoria*. Oxford University Press, 2009.

Tabei, Junko. *Honouring High Places: The Mountain Life of Junko Tabei*. Rocky Mountain Books Ltd, 2017.

Tappenden, Roz. "Ammonite: Who Was the Real Mary Anning?." *BBC News*, 2020, https://www.bbc.com/news/uk-england-dorset-54510746.

Teeter, Emily. "Hatshepsut and Her World." *American Journal of Archeology*, vol 110, 2006, https://www.ajaonline.org/sites/default/files/1104_Teeter.pdf. Accessed 25 Feb 2021.

Tepe, Eric et al. "A New Species of Solanum Named for Jeanne Baret, An Overlooked Contributor to the History of Botany." *Phytokeys*, vol 8, no. 0, 2012, p. 37. Pensoft Publishers, doi:10.3897/phytokeys.8.2101. Accessed 26 Feb 2021.

"The Story of Empress Suiko | Exploring the Footsteps of the Heroines of Asuka." Exploring the Footsteps of the Heroines of Asuka, http://asuka-japan-heritage.jp/global/en/suiko/life/.

Thornton, John K. "Legitimacy and Political Power: Queen Njinga, 1624–1663." *The Journal of African History*, vol 32, no. 01, 1991, p. 25. Cambridge University Press (CUP), doi:10.1017/s0021853700025329. Accessed 7 Mar 2021.

Torrens, Hugh. "Mary Anning (1799–1847) of Lyme; 'The Greatest Fossilist the World Ever Knew.'" *The British Journal for the History of Science*, vol 28, no. 3, 1995, pp. 257–284. Cambridge University Press (CUP), doi:10.1017/s0007087400033161. Accessed 30 Jan 2021.

Townsend, Gloria Childress, et al. "Grace Hopper Visits the Neighborhood." *Proceedings of the 39th SIGCSE Technical Symposium on Computer Science Education—SIGCSE '08*, 2008. ACM Press, doi:10.1145/1352135.1352307. Accessed 30 Jan 2021.

Tracy, James F. "Revisiting a Polysemic Text: The African American Press's Reception of *Gone With the Wind*." *Mass Communication and Society*, vol 4, no. 4, 2001, pp. 419-436. Informa UK Limited, doi:10.1207/s15327825mcs0404_6. Accessed 25 Feb 2021.

Trombetta, Mark. "Madame Maria Sklodowska-Curie—Brilliant Scientist, Humanitarian, Humble Hero: Poland's Gift to the World." *Journal of Contemporary Brachytherapy*, vol 3, 2014, pp. 297–299. Termedia Sp. Z.O.O., doi:10.5114/jcb.2014.45133. Accessed 30 Jan 2021.

Vincent, Peggy et al. "Mary Anning's Legacy to French Vertebrate Palaeontology." *Geological Magazine*, vol 151, no. 1, 2013, pp. 7–20. Cambridge University Press (CUP), doi:10.1017/s0016756813000861. Accessed 30 Jan 2021.

Waldron, Mary. "Jane Austen and the Fiction of Her Time." *Estudios Ingleses De La Universidad Complutense*, vol 2, 2002, https://www.re-searchgate.net/publication/27588718_Jane_Austen_and_the_Fiction_of_her_Time_Mary_Waldron. Accessed 25 Feb 2021.

Walker, Rhiannon. "The Day Alice Coachman Became the First Black Woman to Win Olympic Gold." *The Undefeated*, 2018.

Wallace, Birgitta. "The Norse in Newfoundland: L'Anse Aux Meadows and Vinland." *Newfoundland Studies*, vol 19, no. 1, 2003, Accessed 26 Feb 2021.

"Wangari Maathai. Action for Africa and the Earth." Vol 2, no. 11, 2011, https://www.researchgate.net/publication/316232213_Wangari_Maathai_Action_for_Africa_and_the_Earth. Accessed 26 Feb 2021.

Wentrup, Curt. "Marie Curie, Radioactivity, the Atom, the Neutron, and the Positron." *Australian Journal of Chemistry*, vol 64, no. 7, 2011, p. 847. CSIRO Publishing, doi:10.1071/ch11235. Accessed 30 Jan 2021.

Wheeler, Bonnie, and John Carmi Parsons. *Eleanor of Aquitaine*. Palgrave Macmillan, 2008.

White, Gloria M. "Mary Church Terrell: Organizer of Black Women." *Equity & Excellence in Education*, vol 17, no. 5-6, 1979, pp. 2-8. Informa UK Limited, doi:10.1080/0020486790170501. Accessed 25 Feb 2021.

Wieler, Joachim. "Brief Note: Remembering Irena Sendler." *International Social Work*, vol 51, no. 6, 2008, pp. 835-840. SAGE Publications, doi:10.1177/0020872808095254. Accessed 26 Feb 2021.

Williams, Jane. *"Eat Anywhere": Mary Church Terrell's Quest to End Segregation in the Nation's Capital.* https://www.nhd.org/sites/default/files/WilliamsJrPaper.pdf. Accessed 25 Feb 2021.

"Wilma Rudolph." Biography, 2018, https://www.biography.com/athlete/wilma-rudolph.

Wilson Logan, Shirley. "Frances E. W. Harper, "Woman's Political Future." *Voices of Democracy*, vol 1, 2006, https://voicesofdemocracy.umd.edu/wp-content/uploads/2010/07/logan-harper.pdf. Accessed 25 Feb 2021.

Zanther Carreos, Luisse. "The Diary of a Young Girl: Anne Frank." *Philippine Normal University*, 2016, https://www.researchgate.net/publication/311706117_The_Diary_of_A_Young_Girl_Anne_Frank. Accessed 26 Feb 2021.

Zhang, Zhan. "Cixi and Modernization of China." *Asian Social Science*, vol 6, no. 4, 2010,

https://pdfs.seman-
ticscholar.org/ab45/a2025cdec3c73ce3d5638b0b22bc297b3a84.pdf.
Accessed 25 Feb 2021.

Zielinski, Sarah. "Hypatia, Ancient Alexandria's Great Female
Scholar." *Smithsonian Magazine*, 2010, https://www.smithson-
ianmag.com/history/hypatia-ancient-alexandrias-great-female-
scholar-10942888/.

Thank you for reading my book.

I hope you enjoyed *Extraordinary Women in History*
and have been inspired by these incredible women.

If you liked the book, I would be grateful if you left a review.
It is really important as a self-publisher to get reviews.

You can point your phone camera at the QR code below,
which will take you straight through to Amazon Review.

AMAZON UK	**AMAZON USA**

ABOUT THE AUTHOR

Leah Gail is a Marketeer, Entrepreneur, and Author living in The Cotswolds, UK. Leah's background is in Music Marketing, and having worked in an industry with very few women at the top, she has spent the majority of her time mentoring other women to reach their potential. Leah has also been enlisted in the **Women in Music Roll of Honour**, which recognizes game changers within the industry and has helped other women reach their potential.

Having written *Extraordinary Women in History*, Leah hopes other women will be inspired and encouraged to dream big and let no barriers get in their way.

To keep up to date on other books, you can follow Leah on:

 @leahgailauthor

 @leahgail

Website: leahgail.com

For further information, please sign up to the mailing list: **information@leahgail.co.uk**.

Printed in Great Britain
by Amazon

17204304R00119